I0008599

Title: Insight into Robotics Industries: Insights and Perspectives

Copyright © [2024] by [Mustafa Al-Dori]

Published by [Self-Published]

Contact us:

mustafa.k.mustafa92@gmail.com

Dedication:
For my parents, whose love and guidance shaped my world.

1

About the Author

Dr. Mustafa Kamal Mustafa Al-Dori is a passionate scholar and practitioner in the field of business administration, specializing in marketing. He earned his doctorate from Ain Shams University, Faculty of Business, where he developed a deep understanding of the intricacies of marketing dynamics in today's ever-evolving business landscape.

Despite his academic credentials, Dr. Al-Dori's true passion lies in the practical application of management principles. He has played a pivotal role in numerous projects and has significantly contributed to small and medium-sized enterprises, where his insights and strategies have led to remarkable successes. His experience in the field has equipped him with a unique perspective, bridging the gap between theory and real-world application.

Dr. Al-Dori is also a distinguished speaker at various conferences, where he shares his expertise and innovative ideas. He has contributed to many training programs, empowering aspiring professionals with the knowledge and skills necessary for success in the competitive world of business.

His research work is widely recognized, with several publications in high-impact international journals. Dr. Al-Dori's commitment to advancing the field of marketing is evident in his contributions to academic discourse and his dedication to fostering the next generation of business leaders. Through his work, he continues to inspire others, demonstrating that the fusion of theory and practice is essential for achieving meaningful outcomes in the world of business.

About the Book

Insight into Robotics Industries: Insights and Perspectives provides a comprehensive exploration of the dynamic and rapidly evolving world of robotics. From the history of robotics technology to the future innovations shaping the industry, this book offers a well-rounded understanding of the key aspects that define robotics today.

Designed for professionals, students, and anyone interested in the field, this book delves into critical topics such as:

- **Historical Context and Evolution**: A detailed journey through the key milestones that have shaped the robotics industry, from its inception to the present.

- **Diverse Applications of Robotics**: Insightful analysis into how robotics is transforming sectors like healthcare, agriculture, manufacturing, and logistics, providing real-world examples of its growing influence.

- **Technological Foundations**: An in-depth look at the cutting-edge technologies powering modern robots, including artificial intelligence, machine learning, control systems, and human-robot interaction.

- **Market Trends and Business Perspectives**: An overview of the global robotics market, highlighting key players, strategic partnerships, and emerging startups that are redefining the competitive landscape.

- **Ethical and Regulatory Frameworks**: A critical discussion on the ethical challenges and regulatory policies guiding the development and deployment of robotics technologies across the globe.

- **Future Trends and Opportunities**: An exploration of the future role of robotics in smart cities, sustainability, and the integration of IoT, shedding light on where the industry is headed in the coming decades.

This book serves as both an informative guide and a thought-provoking resource, offering readers a deeper understanding of the opportunities and challenges facing the robotics industry today. Whether you are a researcher, entrepreneur, or simply curious about the future of technology, *Insight into Robotics Industries* is your gateway to comprehending how robotics is reshaping the world around us.

Table of contents

Preface

The robotics industry stands at the forefront of technological advancement, rapidly transforming how we live, work, and interact with the world around us. What was once the realm of science fiction has now become an integral part of daily life, touching industries from healthcare to manufacturing, and agriculture to logistics. Robotics is not just about machines; it's about unlocking new possibilities for efficiency, innovation, and human progress.

As the world faces unprecedented challenges—from global supply chain disruptions to increasing demands for personalized healthcare—robotics holds the promise of addressing many of these issues with novel solutions. This book, *Insight into Robotics Industries: Insights and Perspectives*, was born out of a need to provide a comprehensive understanding of the evolving robotics landscape, and to explore both its history and its future potential.

The journey of writing this book has been one of discovery. I set out not only to inform but also to challenge conventional thinking about robotics. What started as an academic interest soon evolved into a broader exploration of the impact that robots will have on society, the economy, and global markets. Throughout the process, I have engaged with experts in the field, studied technological breakthroughs, and reflected on the ethical questions surrounding robotics—particularly the balance between innovation and societal implications.

This book is organized to offer readers a full picture of the robotics industry. We begin by exploring the origins and historical milestones that have shaped robotics. Then, we dive into the various types of robots and their applications across different sectors. As we progress, you'll encounter discussions on the technologies powering robotics, including artificial intelligence and human-robot interaction, as well as the challenges and opportunities the industry faces.

Writing *Insight into Robotics Industries* has reinforced my belief that collaboration across sectors is essential for driving robotics forward in a responsible and innovative way. It is my hope that this book serves not only as a guide but as a catalyst for future thought, discussion, and discovery in the robotics field.

I would like to extend my deepest thanks to the experts, researchers, and industry leaders who have generously shared their insights and experiences. Their contributions have enriched this book and deepened my understanding of this complex, yet fascinating, domain.

As you embark on this journey through the world of robotics, I encourage you to think beyond the technology itself. Consider the societal impact, the ethical dilemmas, and the collaborative potential that robotics brings to the table. Only through such holistic thinking can we truly harness the power of robotics to shape a better future.

Thank you for joining me in exploring the remarkable world of robotics.

Introduction

The robotics industry is experiencing an unprecedented era of growth, innovation, and transformation. From autonomous drones delivering packages to surgical robots performing delicate operations, robotics has transcended the realm of science fiction to become an integral part of modern society. This book, *Insight into Robotics Industries: Insights and Perspectives*, seeks to explore the vast potential of this rapidly evolving field, while providing a comprehensive analysis of its history, current developments, and future prospects.

Overview of the Robotics Industry

The robotics industry today is a critical pillar of technological advancement. Encompassing a broad range of applications—from industrial automation and healthcare to agriculture and logistics—robotics is revolutionizing the way we live and work. This transformation is being driven by advances in artificial intelligence, machine learning, and sensor technologies, which have enabled robots to become more autonomous, versatile, and intelligent.

Globally, the robotics market is expanding at an extraordinary rate, with industries increasingly adopting robotic solutions to enhance efficiency, productivity, and precision. According to market analysts, the global robotics market is expected to surpass $200 billion by 2026, reflecting its growing importance in sectors as diverse as manufacturing, healthcare, logistics, and even everyday consumer applications. As robotics continues to integrate deeper into society, understanding its development and potential is more critical than ever.

Historical Context and Evolution of Robotics

The journey of robotics has been a fascinating one, marked by key technological breakthroughs and visionary thinkers. The concept of robots has existed for centuries, with early mechanical devices and automata serving as precursors to the sophisticated machines of today. The modern field of robotics, however, took shape in the 20th century, with the invention of industrial robots that revolutionized manufacturing processes.

From early developments like the Unimate, the first industrial robot deployed in a General Motors factory, to the introduction of collaborative robots (cobots) that work alongside humans, robotics has undergone a profound transformation. Advances in computing power, artificial intelligence, and machine learning have further accelerated this evolution, allowing robots to become more capable, adaptable, and intelligent.

This book will trace the historical milestones that have shaped robotics, highlighting the contributions of pioneers in the field and examining the pivotal moments that defined the industry's growth.

Importance of Robotics in Various Sectors

The importance of robotics extends far beyond the manufacturing floor. In the healthcare sector, robots are playing a crucial role in improving patient outcomes, from robotic-assisted surgeries to rehabilitation and caregiving. In agriculture, robotics is enhancing crop yields through precision farming techniques. In logistics, autonomous robots are optimizing supply chain operations, enabling faster, more efficient delivery of goods.

Robotics is also making inroads into more unconventional sectors, such as retail, hospitality, and even entertainment. The diversity of applications illustrates the vast potential of robotics to impact every aspect of human life, making it an indispensable tool for addressing some of the world's most pressing challenges.

Objectives of the Book and Scope of Discussion

The primary objective of this book is to provide readers with a detailed and insightful understanding of the robotics industry. Through a multidisciplinary approach, the book aims to cover various aspects of robotics—from its technological underpinnings and design principles to its real-world applications and ethical considerations. This comprehensive exploration will enable readers to gain a holistic view of the industry, whether they are students, researchers, business professionals, or enthusiasts.

The book is organized into ten chapters, each focusing on a specific area of robotics. It begins with an exploration of the history and evolution of robotics, followed by a discussion on the different types of robots, the technologies that power them, and the design and development processes. Later chapters delve into the applications of robotics across industries, the key players shaping the market, and the regulatory and ethical frameworks that govern the industry. The final chapter addresses future trends, offering insights into the next wave of innovations that will define the future of robotics.

Future Prospects and Challenges in Robotics

The future of robotics is filled with exciting possibilities. With advancements in artificial intelligence, robotics is poised to become even more integrated into everyday life, driving the development of smart cities, autonomous transportation, and intelligent infrastructure. However, with these advancements come significant challenges, including ethical concerns, regulatory hurdles, and the potential for job displacement.

This book will explore these challenges, providing a balanced perspective on both the opportunities and the risks associated with the widespread adoption of robotics. It will also offer a forward-looking view on how the industry can address these challenges through innovation, collaboration, and responsible development.

In conclusion, *Insight into Robotics Industries: Insights and Perspectives* offers a thorough examination of one of the most transformative fields of our time. As we stand on the brink of a new era defined by robotics and automation, this book seeks to inform, inspire, and guide readers through the fascinating world of robots and their potential to reshape our future.

Chapter 1: History of Robotics Technology

1. Early Developments in Robotics
2. Key Milestones in Robotics Evolution
3. Transition from Industrial to Service Robots
4. Major Contributors to Robotics Development
5. Impact of Government Policies and Funding on Robotics Research

Chapter 1

History of Robotics Technology

Introduction

The history of robotics technology is a fascinating journey that spans centuries, beginning with rudimentary mechanical devices and evolving into the highly sophisticated systems that drive today's innovations. This chapter delves into the early developments that laid the foundation for modern robotics, tracing key milestones and pivotal moments that have shaped the field.

From the ancient automata of Greek and Chinese civilizations to the pioneering breakthroughs of the 20th century, the evolution of robotics has been driven by both creative visionaries and technological advances. The transition from industrial robots, which revolutionized manufacturing, to service robots that interact with humans in healthcare, logistics, and daily life, marks a significant turning point in the field.

This chapter also highlights the major contributors to robotics development, including inventors, engineers, and organizations that have played crucial roles in pushing the boundaries of what robots can achieve. Additionally, it examines the impact of government policies and funding on the growth of robotics research, illustrating how strategic investments and regulatory frameworks have accelerated the industry's progress.

By exploring the historical context of robotics, this chapter provides a comprehensive understanding of how the field has matured and sets the stage for discussing the current and future state of robotics technology.

1. Early Developments in Robotics

The concept of robotics has long captured the human imagination, dating back to ancient civilizations and myths that envisioned artificial beings capable of mimicking human actions. Early robotics developments were rooted in mechanical automata, devices created to perform simple tasks without human intervention. These rudimentary machines laid the groundwork for modern robotics, showcasing human ingenuity and a desire to replicate life-like movements through technology.

This section will explore the key early developments in robotics, spanning from ancient automatons to the mechanical innovations of the Renaissance and the industrial era. These foundational steps, though basic compared to today's standards, demonstrate the progression of robotics technology and its eventual evolution into the sophisticated systems of the 20th and 21st centuries.

1.1. Ancient Automata: Early Inspirations

The earliest known examples of robotics can be traced back to ancient civilizations, where automata were created to perform specific tasks. These early robots were not electronic or powered by computers but were mechanical devices operated by gears, water, steam, or human intervention.

One of the most famous examples of ancient automata comes from **Ancient Greece**. The Greek engineer **Hero of Alexandria** (circa 10–70 AD) is often credited with designing a variety of mechanical devices, including self-propelled carts, automated theater productions, and water-powered mechanisms. His work, compiled in texts like *Pneumatica*, demonstrated the potential of basic mechanical systems to perform complex tasks, such as opening doors or simulating movement in figures during religious ceremonies.

Another notable example is from **Ancient China**, where mechanical engineers created automata as early as the 3rd century BCE. **Mozi** and **Lu Ban**, ancient Chinese philosophers and inventors, reportedly constructed wooden birds and other mechanical devices that could move autonomously. These early creations reflect humanity's enduring fascination with machines that mimic natural movements.

1.2. Middle Ages and Renaissance: The Rise of Mechanical Inventions

During the Middle Ages, the development of more sophisticated mechanical devices continued, particularly in Europe. **Islamic scholars** and engineers, such as **Al-Jazari** (1136–1206), made significant contributions to the field of robotics. Al-Jazari, often referred to as the "father of modern robotics," created numerous water-powered devices, including clocks, automata, and mechanical toys. His most notable work, *The Book of Knowledge of Ingenious Mechanical Devices*, documented his inventions, including a humanoid automaton capable of serving drinks at royal banquets.

In the **Renaissance**, mechanical engineering reached new heights, with notable inventors like **Leonardo da Vinci** (1452–1519) contributing to the advancement of robotics. Da Vinci designed several automatons, including a humanoid robot known as the **Leonardo Robot** or the "mechanical knight," which could sit, wave its arms, and even move its head. Although it was never built during his lifetime, modern reconstructions have demonstrated that Da Vinci's designs were highly functional and innovative for their time.

1.3. The 17th to 19th Centuries: The Industrial Revolution and Early Automation

The **Industrial Revolution** marked a turning point in robotics history, as it saw the rise of automation in manufacturing and other industries. This period also witnessed the development of more advanced mechanical devices that would influence later robotic systems.

In the late 18th century, the **Jacquard Loom** was invented by **Joseph Marie Jacquard** (1752–1834). This mechanical loom used punch cards to control the weaving of complex patterns, effectively making it one of the first programmable machines. The Jacquard Loom is considered a precursor to the programmable robots and computers that followed in the 20th century.

Another major advancement during this period was **Charles Babbage's** design for the **Difference Engine** (1822) and the **Analytical Engine** (1837), which were mechanical computing devices capable of performing complex calculations. Although these machines were not completed in Babbage's lifetime, they laid the conceptual foundation for modern computers, which would later be integral to robotics development.

Similarly, the invention of **steam engines** and advances in metallurgy and materials science provided the physical and technological infrastructure necessary for the development of more complex machines.

1.4. The Birth of Modern Robotics: The 20th Century

The 20th century saw the transition from mechanical automation to the first true robots, largely driven by advancements in electrical engineering, computer science, and cybernetics. The term "robot" itself was coined in 1920 by Czech playwright **Karel Čapek** in his play *R.U.R. (Rossum's Universal Robots)*, where humanoid machines were depicted as laborers designed to serve humans. Though Čapek's robots were fictional, the play introduced the concept of machines replacing humans in labor, a theme that would resonate with robotics development for decades to come.

In 1942, the science fiction writer **Isaac Asimov** introduced the **Three Laws of Robotics** in his short story collection *I, Robot*, which explored ethical and practical implications of autonomous robots. While Asimov's laws were fictional, they provided a framework for thinking about the moral and safety concerns surrounding robotics—a conversation that continues to this day.

1.5. Early Mechanical Robots: The Rise of Industry

In the 1950s, the world witnessed the creation of the first industrial robots, which were designed to automate tasks in manufacturing environments. The **Unimate**, developed by **George Devol** and **Joseph Engelberger** in 1954, was the first programmable robot used in an industrial setting. Unimate revolutionized the automotive industry by automating repetitive and hazardous tasks, such as welding and material handling, at **General Motors** factories. This marked the dawn of the robotics revolution in manufacturing, paving the way for widespread adoption in other industries.

The development of **cybernetics** and **artificial intelligence (AI)** in the mid-20th century further propelled robotics technology. **Norbert Wiener**, a pioneer in cybernetics, explored how feedback mechanisms could be used to control machines, leading to the development of more advanced robotic systems that could interact with their environments in real-time.

In the 1960s, the **Stanford Research Institute** developed **Shakey**, the first mobile robot capable of reasoning about its actions. Shakey was able to navigate its environment, perform tasks, and make decisions based on input from sensors. This was a major leap forward in robotics, as it combined automation with artificial intelligence, setting the stage for future advancements in autonomous robots.

1.6. Conclusion: Foundations for Future Robotics

The early developments in robotics, from ancient automata to the first industrial robots, laid the groundwork for the technological advancements we see today. These early inventions showcased human creativity and engineering prowess, demonstrating the potential of machines to perform complex tasks.

As we move into the 21st century, the historical context of robotics provides valuable lessons for understanding the trajectory of modern robotics technology. The innovations of the past continue to influence the field, shaping how robots are designed, developed, and integrated into society.

2. Key Milestones in Robotics Evolution

The evolution of robotics is a rich and complex story that stretches across centuries, involving the convergence of mechanical engineering, electrical systems, and computer science. Each milestone in this journey has pushed the boundaries of what machines can do, from early automatons to today's sophisticated robots. These advancements are not isolated; they have come from the collective effort of scientists, engineers, and researchers across generations and continents. This section traces the key milestones that have shaped the field of robotics, demonstrating how these breakthroughs have laid the foundation for modern robotics technology.

From the development of industrial robots that transformed manufacturing to the rise of autonomous systems that are reshaping healthcare, transportation, and even our homes, each milestone reflects a pivotal moment in the history of robotics. By understanding these historical landmarks, we can appreciate the challenges and innovations that have led to the present-day state of robotics technology.

2.1. The Birth of Modern Robotics: The 1950s and 1960s

One of the earliest and most significant milestones in the history of robotics was the creation of **Unimate** in 1954, the world's first industrial robot, developed by **George Devol** and later commercialized by **Joseph Engelberger**. Unimate was a programmable robotic arm designed for material handling, and its introduction revolutionized the manufacturing industry, particularly in the automotive sector. Installed at a **General Motors** plant in 1961, Unimate automated dangerous and repetitive tasks such as welding and die casting. This marked the beginning of robots replacing human labor in industrial environments, sparking widespread interest in robotic automation.

In the 1960s, robotics research expanded beyond industrial applications. The **Stanford Research Institute** developed **Shakey** in 1966, the first mobile robot that could reason about its actions. Unlike Unimate, which was programmed for specific tasks, Shakey used a combination of sensors and software to navigate its environment and perform tasks independently. Shakey's ability to plan and execute tasks based on sensor data marked a significant leap forward, demonstrating early principles of **artificial intelligence (AI)** in robotics.

2.2. The 1970s: Expanding the Scope of Robotics

The 1970s saw a series of key advancements that expanded the potential applications of robots. In 1973, the first commercially available electric robot, **Famulus**, was developed by the German company **KUKA Robotics**. Famulus featured six electrically driven axes, enabling it to perform more complex and precise tasks than earlier mechanical robots. This advancement reflected the growing role of robotics in precision industries like aerospace and electronics manufacturing.

Another milestone in the 1970s was the development of **PUMA (Programmable Universal Machine for Assembly)**, a robotic arm introduced by **Unimation** and designed specifically for **General Motors** to automate assembly line tasks. PUMA became a standard model for robotic arms and is still used today in various industries, from automotive assembly to medical applications. Its flexibility, programmability, and precision established new benchmarks for what industrial robots could achieve.

The 1970s also marked the rise of robotics in academia and research, with universities like **MIT** and **Stanford** developing robotic systems that incorporated emerging AI technologies. The **Stanford Arm**, developed by **Victor Scheinman** in 1969, was a significant breakthrough, allowing for precise manipulation tasks in various research environments. It laid the foundation for future developments in robotic arms used in both industrial and medical fields.

2.3. The 1980s: Robotics in Space and Medicine

The 1980s saw the introduction of robotics into more specialized and demanding environments, including space exploration and medicine. A major milestone was NASA's development of the **Space Shuttle Remote Manipulator System (SRMS)**, more commonly known as the **Canadarm**. Launched in 1981, the Canadarm was used aboard the **Space Shuttle Columbia** to deploy and retrieve satellites and conduct experiments in space. Its success demonstrated the potential for robotics to operate in hostile and remote environments, laying the groundwork for future space robotics systems like the Mars rovers.

In the field of medicine, the 1980s saw the first use of robotic systems in surgeries. The **Arthrobot**, developed in Canada in 1983, became the first robotic assistant in surgical procedures, performing orthopedic surgeries with high precision. This milestone demonstrated the potential of robotics to revolutionize healthcare by enhancing the accuracy of surgeries and reducing human error.

At the same time, robotics began to gain traction in consumer markets with the development of robotic toys and educational kits. One of the most iconic examples from this era is the **LEGO Mindstorms** kit, introduced in

1984. These kits allowed students and hobbyists to build and program their own robots, sparking interest in robotics among young learners and laying the foundation for the next generation of robotic engineers.

2.4. The 1990s: Autonomous Systems and AI Integration

The 1990s witnessed significant strides in autonomous robotics and the integration of **artificial intelligence (AI)**. A key development during this period was the introduction of **robotic vacuum cleaners**, with **Electrolux** launching the first commercial robotic vacuum, the **Trilobite**, in 1997. While the Trilobite had limitations, it represented the first step toward autonomous robots in domestic environments.

This decade also saw the rise of **mobile robotics**, with research into autonomous vehicles and robotic exploration systems gaining momentum. **Carnegie Mellon University's Navlab** project developed one of the first autonomous ground vehicles capable of navigating complex terrain without human input. This early research contributed to the development of self-driving cars, a technology that would gain prominence in the 21st century.

The 1990s also saw advancements in **robotic prosthetics**, with the development of more sophisticated and responsive systems that could be controlled by neural signals. These technologies not only improved the lives of amputees but also demonstrated the potential for robots to integrate more seamlessly with human biology, a concept that continues to evolve in modern **cyborg** and **bionic limb** research.

2.5. The 2000s: Robotics in Everyday Life

The early 2000s marked a significant shift in robotics, with robots becoming more commonplace in everyday life. The introduction of the **Roomba**, a robotic vacuum cleaner developed by **iRobot** in 2002, brought autonomous robotics into millions of homes. Unlike earlier robotic vacuums, the Roomba was affordable, efficient, and capable of navigating various types of flooring. Its success demonstrated that consumer robotics had matured enough to serve practical purposes in domestic settings.

In addition to household robots, the 2000s saw advancements in **medical robotics**, with systems like the **da Vinci Surgical System** revolutionizing minimally invasive surgeries. The da Vinci system, introduced in 2000, allowed surgeons to perform delicate procedures with enhanced precision and control, reducing recovery times and improving patient outcomes. The success of robotic-assisted surgery in the medical field highlighted the potential for robotics to augment human capabilities in critical areas.

Autonomous robotics also reached new heights in exploration. In 2004, NASA's **Mars Exploration Rovers**, **Spirit** and **Opportunity**, successfully landed on Mars and began their mission to explore the Martian surface. These rovers operated autonomously for extended periods, collecting data and sending it back to Earth. Their success demonstrated the potential for autonomous robots to operate in remote and hostile environments, far beyond the reach of human intervention.

2.6. The 2010s and Beyond: Artificial Intelligence and Robotics Integration

The 2010s marked the convergence of robotics and AI, leading to the development of more intelligent, adaptable, and autonomous systems. Key milestones in this era include the rise of **self-driving cars**, with companies like **Tesla**, **Waymo**, and **Uber** leading the charge in developing fully autonomous vehicles capable of navigating real-world environments. These systems use a combination of sensors, machine learning, and complex algorithms to interpret and react to their surroundings.

Another significant development in the 2010s was the rise of **collaborative robots** or **cobots**, designed to work alongside humans in industrial and service environments. Unlike traditional industrial robots, which operate in isolation due to safety concerns, cobots are equipped with sensors and AI-driven safety protocols that allow them to interact safely with human workers. This innovation has expanded the scope of robotics in industries like manufacturing, logistics, and even healthcare.

The 2010s also saw breakthroughs in **robotic exoskeletons**, which are now being used to help individuals with mobility impairments regain their independence. Companies like **Ekso Bionics** and **ReWalk** have developed exoskeletons that assist with walking and other motor functions, providing a glimpse into the future of human-robot interaction and bionic enhancement.

Conclusion

The milestones discussed in this section illustrate the rapid evolution of robotics technology over the past few decades. From the early industrial robots that revolutionized manufacturing to the integration of AI and autonomous systems in everyday life, each breakthrough has contributed to the growing capabilities of robots. As we look to the future, these milestones will serve as a foundation for even more advanced and intelligent systems that will continue to reshape industries, economies, and societies.

3. Transition from Industrial to Service Robots

The evolution from industrial robots, which largely transformed manufacturing, to service robots, which are impacting sectors like healthcare, education, and hospitality, represents a fundamental shift in robotics applications. While industrial robots have been designed primarily for repetitive and high-precision tasks in controlled environments like factories, service robots have expanded the scope of robotics by interacting directly with humans in dynamic, unstructured environments.

This transition from industrial to service robots is significant not only because of the broader range of applications but also due to the challenges it presents. Service robots must be more adaptable, capable of understanding and reacting to complex human behaviors, and equipped with advanced AI for decision-making. In this section, we will explore how the transition unfolded, examining the key developments, technological innovations, and real-world applications that have facilitated this shift. The impact of service robots on society is profound, and their increasing presence signals a new era in human-robot collaboration.

3.1. The Era of Industrial Robots: Setting the Foundation

Industrial robots, like **Unimate**, developed in the 1960s, were the first robots to be widely used in industry. These machines were designed to automate repetitive tasks such as welding, painting, and assembly in manufacturing plants. The primary focus was on improving productivity and precision while minimizing human involvement in dangerous or labor-intensive tasks. By the 1970s, industrial robots were standard in sectors like automotive manufacturing, with companies such as **General Motors** leading the adoption of these technologies.

These early industrial robots operated in highly structured environments, where the tasks they performed were repetitive and predictable. They followed pre-programmed instructions, had limited flexibility, and were often separated from human workers due to safety concerns. Despite these limitations, industrial robots proved to be highly effective in improving manufacturing efficiency, reducing costs, and ensuring consistent quality in production processes.

The success of industrial robots set the stage for the broader adoption of robotics across different sectors. However, as industries diversified, the need for robots that could operate in less structured environments and interact with humans became apparent. This demand catalyzed the shift from industrial to service robots, driven by advancements in technology such as machine learning, computer vision, and AI.

3.2. Rise of Service Robots: Expanding the Scope

The term "service robot" refers to robots that perform tasks for humans outside of traditional manufacturing environments. These robots are designed to assist people in a wide range of settings, including healthcare, retail, hospitality, education, and even personal care. The rise of service robots began in the late 1990s and early 2000s, when technological advancements made it possible to build robots that could interact with humans and adapt to changing environments.

One of the earliest and most iconic examples of a service robot is the **Roomba**, a robotic vacuum cleaner developed by **iRobot** in 2002. The Roomba was designed for domestic use, offering a simple, automated solution for cleaning floors. It became a commercial success, demonstrating that robots could be useful in everyday life. Unlike industrial robots, which required highly controlled environments, the Roomba was capable of navigating unpredictable home layouts, avoiding obstacles, and adapting to different surfaces.

Another key development in service robotics was the introduction of **robotic assistants** in healthcare. The **da Vinci Surgical System**, introduced in 2000, allowed surgeons to perform minimally invasive surgeries with greater precision and control. This robot-assisted system revolutionized healthcare by improving surgical outcomes and reducing recovery times for patients. In addition to surgical robots, **robotic caregivers** like **PARO**, a therapeutic robot designed to assist with elderly care, demonstrated the potential for robots to provide emotional and physical support in healthcare settings.

The success of these early service robots paved the way for further innovation in robotics applications across various sectors. As demand for personalized, efficient services grew, so did the need for robots capable of more complex interactions with humans.

3.3. Key Technologies Driving the Transition

Several key technological advancements have facilitated the transition from industrial to service robots. These include:

- **Artificial Intelligence (AI) and Machine Learning (ML):** AI and ML have enabled service robots to learn from their environments and improve their performance over time. Unlike industrial robots, which follow pre-programmed instructions, service robots use AI to make real-time decisions based on sensor data, enabling them to interact with humans more effectively. For example, AI allows robots like **Pepper**, developed by **SoftBank Robotics**, to recognize human emotions and respond accordingly in customer service settings.

- **Computer Vision:** The ability to "see" and interpret visual data is crucial for service robots operating in dynamic environments. Computer vision allows robots to identify objects, people, and obstacles in their surroundings, making it possible for them to navigate spaces autonomously. For instance, robots like **Kiva**, used in Amazon's warehouses, rely on computer vision to locate products and optimize storage and retrieval processes.

- **Natural Language Processing (NLP):** NLP enables service robots to understand and respond to human speech, facilitating smoother interactions. This is particularly important in applications like customer service, where robots like **Nina**, a virtual assistant used by **Nuance Communications**, assist customers by answering queries and providing information in a conversational manner.

- **Human-Robot Interaction (HRI):** HRI research focuses on improving the ways humans and robots communicate and collaborate. This field has made significant strides in ensuring that service robots can operate safely around humans, particularly in shared environments like hospitals or homes. **Collaborative robots (cobots)**, which work alongside human workers in manufacturing and healthcare, are a prime example of HRI in action.

- **Robotics Hardware Improvements:** Advances in robotic hardware, including more sophisticated sensors, actuators, and materials, have improved the dexterity, speed, and durability of service robots. This allows robots to perform a wider range of tasks, from precise surgical operations to delicate caregiving activities.

3.4. Applications of Service Robots Across Different Sectors

Service robots are now being deployed in various industries, each requiring different capabilities and technologies. Below are some of the key sectors where service robots have made significant impacts:

- **Healthcare:** In addition to surgical robots like **da Vinci**, robots are being used for patient care, rehabilitation, and even companionship. For example, **Moxi**, a healthcare robot developed by **Diligent Robotics**, assists nurses by delivering supplies, allowing them to spend more time with patients.

- **Hospitality:** Robots are increasingly being used in hotels and restaurants to assist with customer service, room delivery, and even cooking. **Savioke's Relay robot**, for instance, is used in hotels to autonomously deliver items to guests' rooms, improving service efficiency.

- **Retail:** Retailers are using robots to improve customer experiences and streamline operations. **Simbe Robotics' Tally** is a robot that performs inventory management tasks, scanning shelves and notifying store employees of stock shortages or misplaced items. This reduces human error and ensures that products are always available for customers.

- **Education:** In classrooms, robots are being used as teaching assistants to enhance learning experiences. **NAO**, developed by **SoftBank Robotics**, is a humanoid robot used in educational settings to engage students in interactive learning activities, particularly in STEM (Science, Technology, Engineering, and Mathematics) subjects.

- **Logistics and Warehousing:** Service robots are transforming logistics by automating tasks such as picking, packing, and transporting goods. **Kiva Systems**, acquired by Amazon, developed robots that autonomously move products around warehouses, drastically reducing the time and cost associated with manual labor.

- **Personal Assistance and Home Care:** Robots are increasingly being used to assist individuals with disabilities and the elderly. **Jibo**, a social robot, was designed to interact with family members, perform tasks such as setting reminders, and even provide emotional support. Similarly, **Care-O-bot**, developed by the **Fraunhofer Institute**, assists with household tasks for the elderly, promoting independence and improving quality of life.

3.5. Challenges in the Transition from Industrial to Service Robots

While the transition from industrial to service robots has unlocked new possibilities, it also presents several challenges:

- **Human-Robot Interaction:** Service robots must interact with humans in dynamic and unpredictable environments, requiring advanced AI and intuitive interfaces. Ensuring that these robots can understand and respond to human behavior in real time remains a challenge.

- **Safety:** As robots are increasingly deployed in shared spaces, ensuring their safe operation is critical. While industrial robots typically operate in isolated environments, service robots must navigate around people, requiring rigorous safety standards and reliable sensor technologies.

- **Cost:** The cost of developing and deploying service robots remains high, which limits their widespread adoption. Innovations in hardware and software are needed to reduce costs and make these robots accessible to smaller businesses and individuals.

- **Ethical Concerns:** The use of robots in healthcare, eldercare, and education raises ethical questions about the role of robots in human life. Concerns about privacy, job displacement, and the dehumanization of certain services must be addressed as robots become more integrated into daily life.

Conclusion

The transition from industrial to service robots represents a significant leap in robotics technology and its applications. While industrial robots revolutionized manufacturing, service robots are poised to transform a much broader array of sectors, from healthcare to hospitality. With advances in AI, machine learning, computer vision, and human-robot interaction, service robots are becoming more capable of performing complex tasks and interacting with humans in meaningful ways.

As the field of robotics continues to evolve, the challenges of safety, cost, and ethics will need to be addressed to ensure that service robots can achieve their full potential. Nonetheless, the progress made so far suggests that service robots will play an increasingly important role in the future of work, healthcare, education, and daily life.

4. Major Contributors to Robotics Development

The development of robotics as a field has been influenced by a multitude of pioneers, engineers, researchers, and organizations across the globe. These contributors have shaped the trajectory of robotics through innovative designs, groundbreaking research, and the establishment of standards that govern robotic technologies. Their combined efforts have paved the way for advancements in both industrial and service robots, making them integral to modern society.

In this chapter, we will explore the major contributors to robotics development, highlighting their significant achievements and contributions to the field. From early inventors who laid the groundwork for robotic technology to contemporary leaders who drive innovation, we will examine how these individuals and organizations have transformed the landscape of robotics. By analyzing their contributions, we can gain insights into the challenges faced, the solutions developed, and the future direction of robotics as a discipline.

4.1. Early Pioneers in Robotics

The history of robotics can be traced back to ancient civilizations, where myths and legends featured mechanical beings. However, the modern concept of robotics began to take shape in the 20th century. Key figures in early robotics include:

- **George Devol (1912-2011)**: Often regarded as the father of industrial robotics, George Devol invented the first programmable robot, **Unimate**, in the late 1950s. This robot was designed for repetitive tasks in manufacturing, such as welding and material handling. Devol's invention laid the foundation for the robotics industry and demonstrated the potential for automation in manufacturing processes.

- **Isaac Asimov (1920-1992)**: Though not a robotics engineer, Asimov's science fiction writing introduced the world to the concept of robotics and artificial intelligence. His "Three Laws of Robotics" outlined ethical guidelines for robot behavior, influencing how engineers and researchers approached robot design and interaction with humans. Asimov's work ignited public interest in robotics and inspired future generations of engineers.

- **Victor Scheinman (1942-present)**: Scheinman was instrumental in the development of the **Stanford**

Arm, one of the first computer-controlled robotic arms. Introduced in the late 1960s, the Stanford Arm was pivotal in advancing robotic manipulation and paved the way for modern robotic arms used in various applications, from industrial automation to surgery.

4.2. Contributions from Academia and Research Institutions

The academic community has played a crucial role in advancing robotics research and development. Several universities and research institutions have made significant contributions to the field:

- **Massachusetts Institute of Technology (MIT)**: MIT has been a hub for robotics research, producing numerous influential projects and inventions. The **MIT Media Lab** has developed robots like **Kismet**, a socially interactive robot that can recognize and respond to human emotions, and **Cheetah**, a fast-running robot that mimics the movements of its namesake.

- **Carnegie Mellon University (CMU)**: CMU's Robotics Institute is renowned for its research in robot perception, navigation, and machine learning. The development of the **Tartan Racing** team, which created **Boss**, an autonomous vehicle that won the 2007 DARPA Urban Challenge, exemplifies CMU's contributions to the field.

- **Stanford University**: Stanford has produced influential research in robotics, particularly in human-robot interaction. The **Harker School's Robotics Team** has developed robots capable of performing tasks in real-world environments, contributing to advancements in mobile robotics and autonomous systems.

4.3. Notable Organizations and Companies

Several companies have emerged as key players in the robotics industry, driving innovation and commercialization of robotic technologies. Notable organizations include:

- **iRobot**: Founded by Rodney Brooks, Colin Angle, and Helen Greiner in 1990, iRobot is best known for creating the **Roomba**, a robotic vacuum cleaner that revolutionized household cleaning. The company's commitment to developing intelligent robots for everyday tasks has made a significant impact on the consumer robotics market.

- **Boston Dynamics**: Known for its advanced robotic systems, Boston Dynamics has developed robots such as **BigDog**, a quadruped robot designed for military applications, and **Atlas**, a humanoid robot capable of navigating complex environments. Their work emphasizes dynamic mobility and advanced robotic capabilities.

- **FANUC**: A leader in industrial robotics, FANUC specializes in automation technology for manufacturing. The company has produced a wide range of robotic arms used in assembly, welding, and painting, significantly improving production efficiency in various industries.

- **ABB**: ABB is a global leader in power and automation technologies, and its robotics division focuses on providing innovative solutions for industrial automation. ABB robots are widely used in manufacturing, particularly in the automotive sector, contributing to increased efficiency and productivity.

4.4. Influential Researchers and Innovators

Numerous researchers and innovators have made substantial contributions to the theoretical and practical aspects of robotics. Their work has advanced our understanding of robotic systems and their applications:

- **Rodney Brooks**: A pioneer in robotics and AI, Brooks co-founded iRobot and served as the director of the MIT Media Lab. He developed the **subsumption architecture**, a revolutionary approach to robot control that allows robots to react to their environment in real time, paving the way for more autonomous systems.

- **Hans Moravec**: An influential roboticist and researcher, Moravec is known for his work on robot perception and autonomous navigation. His predictions about the future of robotics and AI have inspired ongoing research in the field.

- **RoboCup and Competitions**: Events like **RoboCup**, established in 1997, have fostered innovation and collaboration among researchers and students. The annual competition focuses on advancing robotics and AI by challenging teams to develop autonomous robots capable of playing soccer. These competitions have led to significant advancements in robot perception, coordination, and teamwork.

4.5. Global Collaborations and Initiatives

International collaborations and initiatives have also played a significant role in advancing robotics research and development. Notable efforts include:

- **The European Union's Horizon 2020 Program**: This initiative supports research and innovation in robotics, fostering collaboration between academia and industry across Europe. Projects funded under Horizon 2020 have focused on developing advanced robotic systems for various applications, from healthcare to agriculture.

- **NASA's Robotics Programs**: NASA has been at the forefront of robotics in space exploration. Programs such as the **Mars Rover** missions have demonstrated the capabilities of autonomous robots in extreme environments, paving the way for future exploration of other planets.

- **International Federation of Robotics (IFR)**: The IFR promotes robotics globally by providing insights into market trends, statistics, and research. Its efforts to bring together industry stakeholders and researchers have helped shape the future of robotics worldwide.

Conclusion

The evolution of robotics is a testament to the collaborative efforts of numerous individuals, organizations, and institutions. From early pioneers who laid the groundwork to contemporary innovators driving technological advancements, each contributor has played a vital role in shaping the field. As robotics continues to advance, the contributions of these key figures will remain foundational in navigating the challenges and opportunities that lie ahead.

5. Impact of Government Policies and Funding on Robotics Research

Government policies and funding play a pivotal role in shaping the landscape of robotics research and development. Through strategic investments and supportive regulations, governments can foster innovation, drive technological advancements, and promote the integration of robotics across various sectors. In this chapter, we will explore the impact of government initiatives on robotics research, examining how funding, regulatory frameworks, and public-private partnerships contribute to the growth and evolution of the field.

Government investments in robotics have the potential to stimulate economic growth, enhance workforce capabilities, and improve quality of life through automation and intelligent systems. Additionally, supportive policies can help address the ethical and social implications of robotics, ensuring that technological advancements align with public interests and safety standards. By analyzing various government initiatives, funding programs, and their outcomes, we can gain insights into the essential role that governmental support plays in the future of robotics.

5.1. Government Funding Initiatives

Government funding initiatives are crucial for advancing robotics research and development. These initiatives can take various forms, including grants, contracts, and collaborative research programs. Key examples include:

- **National Science Foundation (NSF) - USA**: The NSF has been a significant source of funding for robotics research in the United States. Through its **Robotics Program**, the NSF supports academic and industrial research aimed at developing innovative robotic technologies. Notable funded projects include those focused on autonomous vehicles, robotic manipulation, and human-robot interaction.

- **European Union's Horizon 2020 Program**: The Horizon 2020 program is one of the largest research and innovation funding programs globally, with a significant focus on robotics. The initiative allocates substantial resources to projects that promote robotics in various sectors, including healthcare, manufacturing, and agriculture. For example, projects like **RoboHealth** aim to develop robotic solutions for patient care, highlighting the program's commitment to enhancing healthcare through technology.

- **Advanced Robotics for Manufacturing (ARM) Institute - USA**: The ARM Institute is a public-private partnership that focuses on accelerating the adoption of robotics in manufacturing. Funded by the U.S. government and industry partners, the institute promotes collaborative research and development projects that address critical challenges in the manufacturing sector, such as workforce training and automation integration.

- **Japan's Robot Revolution Initiative**: In response to an aging population and labor shortages, the Japanese government launched the **Robot Revolution Initiative** in 2015. This program aims to promote robotics in various sectors, including healthcare and agriculture, by providing funding for research, development, and deployment of robotic solutions. The initiative has led to the development of assistive robots for elderly care and agricultural robots for improved crop management.

5.2. Regulatory Frameworks and Standards

Government policies also shape the regulatory frameworks that govern robotics research and deployment. Establishing clear standards and guidelines is essential for ensuring the safe and ethical use of robotic technologies. Key aspects include:

- **Safety Standards**: Governments often establish safety standards for robotic systems to minimize risks associated with their deployment. For instance, the **ISO 10218** standard developed by the International Organization for Standardization (ISO) provides guidelines for the safety of industrial robots. Compliance with such standards helps ensure the safe operation of robots in manufacturing environments.

- **Ethical Considerations**: Governments must also address the ethical implications of robotics, particularly concerning issues such as job displacement, privacy, and accountability. In 2019, the European Commission published guidelines for the ethical development and use of AI and robotics, emphasizing the importance of transparency, fairness, and human oversight in robotic systems.

- **Liability and Accountability**: As robots become more autonomous, questions of liability and accountability arise in case of accidents or malfunctions. Governments are tasked with creating legal frameworks that address these issues, ensuring that responsibility is clearly defined and that victims can seek redress when necessary.

- **Cross-Border Collaboration**: Robotics research often involves international collaboration, necessitating harmonized regulations and standards across borders. Initiatives like the **Global Robotics Alliance** aim to facilitate cooperation between countries in developing standards and sharing best practices in robotics research.

5.3. Public-Private Partnerships

Public-private partnerships (PPPs) are instrumental in advancing robotics research by leveraging resources and expertise from both sectors. Key examples include:

- **Defense Advanced Research Projects Agency (DARPA) - USA**: DARPA has a long history of funding and supporting robotics research with applications in national security. Programs such as the **DARPA Robotics Challenge** have encouraged collaboration between academic institutions and private companies to develop advanced robotic systems for disaster response and search-and-rescue missions.

- **UK Robotics and Autonomous Systems (RAS) Strategy**: The UK government launched the RAS strategy to promote the growth of the robotics sector in collaboration with industry partners. This strategy focuses on key areas such as healthcare, agriculture, and transport, facilitating partnerships between academia, industry, and government to drive innovation and commercialization of robotic technologies.

- **Singapore's Smart Nation Initiative**: Singapore's government has prioritized robotics as part of its **Smart Nation Initiative**, promoting public-private partnerships to drive innovation in robotics. The initiative encourages collaboration between government agencies, research institutions, and private companies to develop solutions for urban challenges, including mobility and healthcare.

- **China's Robotics Industry Development Plan**: The Chinese government has made significant investments in robotics through its **Robotics Industry Development Plan**. This initiative promotes collaboration between state-owned enterprises and private companies, aiming to establish China as a global leader in robotics by fostering innovation and commercialization of advanced robotic technologies.

5.4. Societal Impacts of Government Policies

Government policies and funding have far-reaching societal impacts, influencing the adoption and acceptance of robotic technologies. Key considerations include:

- **Workforce Development**: As robotics continues to reshape industries, governments play a crucial role in preparing the workforce for the changing job landscape. Funding for education and training programs in robotics and automation is essential to equip workers with the necessary skills. Initiatives such as **Code.org** in the United States focus on promoting STEM education and robotics training in schools.

- **Public Awareness and Acceptance**: Government initiatives can also help raise public awareness about the benefits and challenges of robotics. By promoting transparent communication and education campaigns, governments can foster public acceptance of robotic technologies. For instance, the **European Commission** has launched initiatives to inform citizens about AI and robotics, emphasizing their potential benefits for society.

- **Ethical and Social Implications**: Governments are tasked with addressing the ethical and social implications of robotics deployment. By establishing ethical guidelines and promoting responsible innovation, governments can help ensure that technological advancements align with societal values and priorities.

- **Addressing Inequality**: The deployment of robotics can exacerbate existing inequalities if not managed carefully. Governments must implement policies that ensure equitable access to the benefits of robotics, particularly in underserved communities. This includes funding initiatives that promote access to robotics education and technology for marginalized groups.

Conclusion

The impact of government policies and funding on robotics research and development is profound and multifaceted. Through strategic investments, regulatory frameworks, and public-private partnerships, governments can foster innovation and drive the adoption of robotic technologies across various sectors. As the field of robotics continues to evolve, ongoing government support will be essential in addressing the challenges and opportunities that lie ahead, ensuring that robotics contributes positively to society and the economy.

Chapter 2: Types of Robotics

1. Classification of Robotics (Industrial, Service, Collaborative, etc.)
2. Differences Between Autonomous and Semi-Autonomous Robots
3. Emerging Trends in Robotics Applications
4. Robotics in Agriculture, Healthcare, and Manufacturing
5. Future Classifications and Innovations in Robotics

Chapter 2

Types of Robotics

Introduction

The field of robotics encompasses a diverse range of technologies and applications, each tailored to meet specific needs and challenges across various sectors. This chapter delves into the different classifications of robotics, providing a comprehensive overview of the various types and their unique characteristics. Understanding these classifications is essential for grasping the vast potential of robotics in transforming industries and improving everyday life.

Robotics can be broadly categorized into several types, including industrial robots, service robots, collaborative robots, and many others. Each category serves distinct purposes and operates within specific environments, reflecting the versatility and adaptability of robotic technologies. Moreover, the distinction between autonomous and semi-autonomous robots highlights the varying levels of human intervention required in their operation, further illustrating the spectrum of robotic capabilities.

As technology advances, emerging trends in robotics applications are reshaping industries such as agriculture, healthcare, and manufacturing. These innovations not only enhance efficiency and productivity but also pave the way for new possibilities in automation and problem-solving. The future of robotics holds even more promise, with ongoing research and development leading to new classifications and innovations that will continue to revolutionize how we live and work.

In this chapter, we will explore each classification of robotics in detail, examine the differences between autonomous and semi-autonomous robots, and discuss emerging trends and future innovations. By understanding these concepts, readers will gain valuable insights into the transformative impact of robotics across various sectors and the exciting possibilities that lie ahead.

1. Classification of Robotics (Industrial, Service, Collaborative, etc.)

The classification of robotics serves as the foundational framework for understanding the myriad applications and capabilities of robotic technologies in contemporary society. Robotics, as an interdisciplinary field, spans across various domains, with each classification addressing specific challenges and requirements inherent to those domains. This section aims to dissect the classifications of robotics into distinct categories, focusing primarily on industrial robots, service robots, collaborative robots, and other emerging types. By exploring these classifications, readers will gain a clearer understanding of the versatility and functionality of robots in various sectors.

The importance of classifying robots stems from the diverse environments in which they operate and the tasks they perform. For instance, industrial robots are predominantly used in manufacturing processes to enhance productivity, while service robots are increasingly becoming integral in daily life, performing tasks ranging from cleaning to healthcare assistance. Collaborative robots, or cobots, represent a significant evolution in the robotics field, as they are designed to work alongside humans, blending human intelligence with robotic efficiency.

This chapter will provide an in-depth analysis of each classification, highlighting their characteristics, applications, and real-world examples that demonstrate their impact. The discussion will not only encompass traditional classifications but also address the emerging trends in robotics that are reshaping how we think about automation and robotic integration in various sectors.

1.1 Industrial Robots

Definition and Characteristics

Industrial robots are automated machines designed to perform specific tasks in manufacturing and production environments. Typically, these robots are programmed to carry out repetitive tasks with high precision, speed, and efficiency, making them indispensable in modern manufacturing processes. They are commonly used for welding, painting, assembly, pick and place, packaging, and product inspection.

Examples

One prominent example of industrial robots is the **KUKA KR 100**, a six-axis robot used in automotive manufacturing for tasks such as welding and assembly. The KR 100 is known for its speed and precision, enabling manufacturers to streamline production processes and reduce labor costs.

Another example is the **ABB IRB 6700**, a versatile industrial robot used for a variety of applications, including material handling and machine tending. Its flexibility allows it to adapt to different tasks, making it a popular choice in industries such as automotive, electronics, and food processing.

Advantages of Industrial Robots

- **Increased Productivity:** Industrial robots can operate continuously without fatigue, significantly increasing production rates.

- **Consistency and Quality:** Robots perform tasks with high precision, reducing the likelihood of defects and ensuring consistent quality.

- **Safety:** By automating dangerous tasks, industrial robots help to reduce workplace accidents and enhance worker safety.

1.2 Service Robots

Definition and Characteristics

Service robots are designed to assist humans by performing tasks in non-manufacturing environments. These robots can operate autonomously or semi-autonomously, providing a wide range of services in sectors such as healthcare, hospitality, and domestic assistance.

Examples

A notable example of a service robot is the **iRobot Roomba**, a robotic vacuum cleaner that autonomously navigates and cleans floors. The Roomba utilizes sensors to avoid obstacles and efficiently clean various floor surfaces, making it a popular choice for households worldwide.

In the healthcare sector, the **Da Vinci Surgical System** exemplifies a service robot that assists surgeons during minimally invasive procedures. The system enhances precision and control, allowing surgeons to perform complex surgeries with improved outcomes.

Advantages of Service Robots

- **Enhanced Convenience:** Service robots simplify tasks for users, freeing up time for more important activities.

- **Improved Efficiency:** These robots can perform tasks quickly and accurately, improving overall service delivery.

- **Assistance in Critical Situations:** In healthcare, service robots can support medical professionals, providing assistance in surgery or patient care.

1.3 Collaborative Robots (Cobots)

Definition and Characteristics

Collaborative robots, or cobots, are designed to work alongside humans in a shared workspace. Unlike traditional industrial robots that operate in isolation, cobots are equipped with safety features that allow them to interact safely with human workers. This collaboration enhances productivity while maintaining a safe working environment.

Examples

One of the leading examples of collaborative robots is the **Universal Robots UR10**, which is widely used in manufacturing for tasks such as assembly, packaging, and palletizing. Its lightweight design and user-friendly programming make it accessible to a variety of industries.

Another example is the **RoboCup**, a collaborative robot that assists in logistics and warehousing operations. By working alongside human workers, RoboCup optimizes workflows and reduces manual labor.

Advantages of Collaborative Robots

- **Flexibility:** Cobots can be easily reprogrammed and deployed for different tasks, making them versatile in dynamic environments.

- **Increased Human-Robot Interaction:** Cobots enhance collaboration between human workers and robots, fostering a more integrated workforce.

- **Cost-Effectiveness:** Collaborative robots are often less expensive than traditional industrial robots, making automation more accessible for small and medium-sized enterprises.

1.4 Other Emerging Types of Robots

In addition to industrial, service, and collaborative robots, several emerging types of robots are gaining traction in various sectors. These include:

- **Humanoid Robots:** Designed to resemble humans in appearance and behavior, humanoid robots are used in research, entertainment, and customer service applications. Examples include **Sophia**, a social humanoid robot developed by Hanson Robotics.

- **Autonomous Mobile Robots (AMRs):** These robots navigate their environment using sensors and artificial intelligence, allowing them to perform tasks such as delivery and inventory management. An example is the **Amazon Robotics Kiva**, which automates warehouse logistics.

- **Drones:** Unmanned aerial vehicles (UAVs) are increasingly used in various applications, including agriculture, surveillance, and delivery services. For example, **DJI's Phantom series** is widely used for aerial photography and surveying.

Conclusion

The classification of robotics provides a comprehensive understanding of the various types of robots and their respective applications across industries. From industrial robots that drive manufacturing efficiency to service robots that enhance everyday life, each classification contributes significantly to the advancement of automation. Collaborative robots represent a new era of human-robot interaction, highlighting the potential for synergy between human intelligence and robotic efficiency. As technology continues to evolve, emerging types of robots will further expand the horizons of robotics, paving the way for innovative applications that will shape the future of various sectors.

2. Differences Between Autonomous and Semi-Autonomous Robots

The landscape of robotics is characterized by a diverse range of machines designed to perform tasks that can vary significantly in complexity and autonomy. Among these, two primary categories have emerged: autonomous and semi-autonomous robots. Understanding the differences between these two classifications is crucial for appreciating their respective applications, capabilities, and limitations.

Autonomous robots are designed to operate independently without human intervention, relying on advanced algorithms, sensors, and artificial intelligence (AI) to navigate and perform tasks in real-time. These robots can make decisions based on their programming and the data they gather from their environment. Conversely, semi-autonomous robots require human oversight or intervention for certain functions, blending autonomy with human control.

This chapter will delve into the defining characteristics of both autonomous and semi-autonomous robots, highlighting their operational frameworks, use cases, and technological underpinnings. By examining real-world examples and applications, readers will gain a deeper understanding of how these robots function and their implications for various industries.

2.1 Defining Autonomous Robots

Characteristics of Autonomous Robots

Autonomous robots are characterized by their ability to operate independently. They are equipped with sophisticated sensors, such as cameras, LiDAR, and ultrasonic sensors, which allow them to perceive their surroundings. This sensory data is processed using advanced algorithms to make real-time decisions, enabling the robot to navigate and execute tasks without human intervention.

Examples of Autonomous Robots

- **Self-Driving Cars:** One of the most well-known examples of autonomous robots is self-driving cars, such as those developed by Waymo and Tesla. These vehicles utilize a combination of sensors, cameras, and AI algorithms to navigate roads, recognize traffic signals, and avoid obstacles without human input.

- **Autonomous Drones:** Drones like the **DJI Phantom 4** can autonomously fly predetermined flight paths, capturing aerial images and videos. They can adjust their flight patterns based on real-time data from their sensors.

Advantages of Autonomous Robots

- **Efficiency:** Autonomous robots can operate continuously, optimizing processes without the need for breaks or human supervision.

- **Consistency:** Their ability to perform tasks without fatigue ensures consistent quality in outputs, particularly in manufacturing and logistics.

- **Safety:** By automating dangerous tasks, autonomous robots reduce the risk of human injury in hazardous environments, such as disaster response situations.

2.2 Defining Semi-Autonomous Robots

Characteristics of Semi-Autonomous Robots

Semi-autonomous robots operate with a combination of automated processes and human oversight. While they can perform certain tasks independently, they often require human intervention for decision-making, especially in complex or unpredictable environments. This type of robot typically includes features that enable human operators to guide, control, or override the robot's actions when necessary.

Examples of Semi-Autonomous Robots

- **Telepresence Robots:** Devices like the **Double Robotics** telepresence robot allow users to interact with others in a remote location. While the robot can navigate autonomously within a set area, a human operator controls its movements and interactions through a remote interface.

- **Military Drones:** Unmanned Aerial Vehicles (UAVs), such as the **MQ-9 Reaper**, exemplify semi-autonomous robots. These drones can carry out missions autonomously but often require human pilots to make critical decisions during complex operations.

Advantages of Semi-Autonomous Robots

- **Human Oversight:** The involvement of human operators allows for greater adaptability in unpredictable environments, where human judgment is crucial.

- **Flexibility:** Semi-autonomous robots can switch between automated functions and manual control, enabling them to handle a wider range of tasks.

- **Safety Net:** In situations where autonomous robots might encounter obstacles or unforeseen circumstances, human intervention can prevent accidents and ensure safety.

2.3 Key Differences Between Autonomous and Semi-Autonomous Robots

Operational Independence

- **Autonomous Robots:** Operate completely independently and make decisions based on their programming and sensor data without human intervention.

- **Semi-Autonomous Robots:** Require human input or control for certain functions, especially in complex scenarios, blending autonomy with human oversight.

Complexity of Tasks

- **Autonomous Robots:** Capable of performing complex tasks without assistance, such as navigating a city or conducting search and rescue missions.

- **Semi-Autonomous Robots:** Often limited to simpler tasks that can be automated, with the human operator providing guidance for more complex operations.

Decision-Making Processes

- **Autonomous Robots:** Utilize algorithms and AI to make real-time decisions based on data from their environment.

- **Semi-Autonomous Robots:** Rely on human operators to make critical decisions, particularly in dynamic or uncertain situations.

Applications

- **Autonomous Robots:** Commonly used in environments where tasks are repetitive and predictable, such as manufacturing, logistics, and exploration.

- **Semi-Autonomous Robots:** Found in applications requiring human judgment, such as healthcare (e.g., robotic surgery assistants) and telepresence.

2.4 Future Directions in Robotics Autonomy

The ongoing advancements in AI, machine learning, and robotics technology are shaping the future of both autonomous and semi-autonomous robots. As these technologies continue to evolve, the line between the two classifications may blur, leading to more sophisticated robots capable of handling increasingly complex tasks with minimal human intervention.

- **Enhanced AI Capabilities:** Future autonomous robots will benefit from improved AI algorithms that allow for better decision-making in unpredictable environments, enhancing their operational capabilities.

- **Integration of Human-Robot Collaboration:** Semi-autonomous robots will become more adept at collaborating with humans, leading to safer and more efficient workflows in industries like manufacturing and healthcare.

- **Regulatory and Ethical Considerations:** As robots become more autonomous, ethical considerations and regulatory frameworks will need to evolve to address issues of accountability, safety, and the implications of automation on employment.

Conclusion

Understanding the differences between autonomous and semi-autonomous robots is essential for recognizing their respective roles and applications in various industries. Autonomous robots exemplify the pinnacle of robotic independence, performing tasks without human intervention, while semi-autonomous robots offer a hybrid approach that combines automation with human oversight. As technology advances, the interplay between these two classifications will continue to shape the future of robotics, driving innovation and expanding the horizons of automation.

3. Emerging Trends in Robotics Applications

The field of robotics is experiencing rapid growth and transformation, driven by advancements in technology, artificial intelligence, and machine learning. These developments are paving the way for innovative applications across various industries, significantly altering the landscape of work and everyday life. This chapter explores the emerging trends in robotics applications, highlighting their impact on sectors such as healthcare, manufacturing, agriculture, and more.

As robots evolve from being simple machines that execute repetitive tasks to intelligent systems capable of complex problem-solving, they are becoming indispensable tools in addressing modern challenges. The integration of robotics with other technologies, such as the Internet of Things (IoT) and big data analytics, is further enhancing their capabilities and expanding their potential uses. By examining the latest trends in robotics applications, this chapter aims to provide insights into the future trajectory of this dynamic field.

3.1 Robotics in Healthcare

Innovative Surgical Robots

The healthcare sector is one of the most significant beneficiaries of robotics technology. Surgical robots, such as the **da Vinci Surgical System**, have revolutionized minimally invasive surgeries. These robots enhance precision, reduce recovery times, and minimize the risk of complications. Surgeons can control these robotic systems with great accuracy, allowing for complex procedures to be performed with enhanced dexterity.

Rehabilitation Robots

Robotic exoskeletons are increasingly being used in rehabilitation therapy for patients with mobility impairments. For example, the **EksoGT** exoskeleton enables patients with spinal cord injuries or strokes to regain the ability to walk through assisted movement. These devices not only enhance physical recovery but also improve patients' psychological well-being by restoring their mobility.

Telemedicine and Remote Surgery

Telepresence robots have emerged as vital tools for remote consultations and surgeries, especially in rural or underserved areas. These robots allow doctors to examine patients and perform surgeries remotely, ensuring that quality healthcare is accessible to all. For instance, the **InTouch Health** system enables physicians to provide real-time consultations and monitor patients from a distance, significantly enhancing the reach of medical expertise.

3.2 Robotics in Manufacturing

Smart Factories and Automation

The rise of Industry 4.0 has brought about the concept of smart factories, where robotics plays a crucial role in automating production processes. Collaborative robots, or cobots, are designed to work alongside human workers, enhancing productivity and safety. For example, **Universal Robots** has developed cobots that can be easily programmed to perform repetitive tasks, freeing human workers to focus on more complex responsibilities.

Predictive Maintenance

Robots equipped with AI and IoT sensors can monitor machinery in real time, predicting maintenance needs before failures occur. This proactive approach minimizes downtime and maintenance costs. Companies like **Siemens** are leveraging these technologies to optimize their production lines, ensuring efficiency and reliability in operations.

Quality Control and Inspection

Robots are also being employed for quality control in manufacturing processes. Automated inspection systems utilize machine vision technology to detect defects in products with higher accuracy than human inspectors. For instance, **Cognex** produces vision systems that enable manufacturers to ensure their products meet stringent quality standards, thereby reducing waste and increasing customer satisfaction.

3.3 Robotics in Agriculture

Precision Farming

Robots are transforming the agricultural sector through precision farming techniques. Automated systems can monitor crop health, soil conditions, and weather patterns, allowing farmers to make informed decisions. Drones, such as those developed by **DJI**, are used for aerial imaging and mapping, providing farmers with real-time data to optimize crop yields.

Automated Harvesting

Harvesting robots, such as the **Agrobot**, are designed to autonomously pick fruits and vegetables. These robots are equipped with advanced sensors and AI algorithms that enable them to identify ripe produce and harvest it without damaging the plants. This technology is particularly beneficial in addressing labor shortages in agriculture, ensuring timely harvesting and reducing waste.

Livestock Monitoring

Robotics is also enhancing livestock management through automated monitoring systems. Devices like the **Lely Astronaut** milking robot allow farmers to milk cows without manual intervention, improving efficiency and animal welfare. These systems monitor each cow's health and milk production, enabling farmers to make data-driven decisions regarding their livestock.

3.4 Robotics in Logistics and Supply Chain Management

Autonomous Delivery Robots

The rise of e-commerce has led to the development of autonomous delivery robots. Companies like **Starship Technologies** have introduced small, ground-based robots that can deliver groceries and packages to customers' doorsteps. These robots navigate sidewalks and streets, demonstrating the potential for robotics to streamline last-mile delivery processes.

Warehouse Automation

Robotic systems are increasingly used in warehouses to automate picking, packing, and sorting processes. For instance, **Amazon** employs Kiva robots to transport goods within its fulfillment centers, significantly increasing efficiency and reducing operational costs. These robots can work alongside human workers, creating a seamless integration of human and robotic labor.

Inventory Management

Robotic solutions are also being developed for inventory management. Drones and ground-based robots equipped with RFID technology can conduct inventory checks in warehouses, ensuring that stock levels are accurately monitored and maintained. This automation reduces human error and enhances overall operational efficiency.

3.5 Emerging Robotics Technologies

Artificial Intelligence and Machine Learning

The integration of AI and machine learning is a significant trend in robotics, enabling robots to learn from their experiences and adapt to new environments. This capability enhances their autonomy and decision-making abilities, making them more versatile and effective in various applications.

Swarm Robotics

Inspired by nature, swarm robotics involves the coordination of multiple robots to accomplish tasks collectively. This approach can be applied in areas such as environmental monitoring, search and rescue operations, and agricultural tasks. For example, a swarm of drones can work together to monitor large agricultural fields, collecting data on crop health and growth patterns.

Human-Robot Interaction

Advancements in human-robot interaction technologies are improving the ways in which robots communicate and collaborate with humans. Natural language processing (NLP) and gesture recognition are being integrated into robotic systems, enabling more intuitive and seamless interactions. This trend is particularly relevant in sectors like healthcare, where robots can assist patients and caregivers more effectively.

Conclusion

The emerging trends in robotics applications reflect the rapid evolution of technology and its potential to transform various sectors. From healthcare and manufacturing to agriculture and logistics, robots are increasingly becoming integral to modern workflows. As advancements in AI, machine learning, and human-robot interaction continue to progress, the future of robotics holds exciting possibilities for innovation and efficiency across industries.

4. Robotics in Agriculture, Healthcare, and Manufacturing

Robotics has emerged as a transformative technology across various sectors, fundamentally changing how industries operate. In agriculture, healthcare, and manufacturing, robots enhance efficiency, improve precision, and enable new levels of productivity. As these industries face increasing demands for higher quality, faster output, and cost-effectiveness, robotics provides innovative solutions that address these challenges.

This chapter explores the applications of robotics in agriculture, healthcare, and manufacturing, highlighting specific examples of how these technologies are being utilized. By examining the benefits and advancements in each sector, we can gain insights into the critical role of robotics in shaping the future of work and improving quality of life.

4.1 Robotics in Agriculture

Precision Agriculture

Precision agriculture, which utilizes robotics and technology to optimize field-level management, is revolutionizing farming practices. Drones equipped with imaging sensors can survey large areas of farmland, collecting data on crop health and soil conditions. For instance, **DJI's Phantom 4 RTK** drone provides high-resolution images that enable farmers to monitor crop stress, leading to more efficient use of water and fertilizers.

Automated Harvesting Systems

The labor-intensive nature of harvesting fruits and vegetables poses challenges for farmers, particularly during peak seasons. Robotic harvesters, such as the **Agrobot**, are designed to autonomously pick crops. These robots use advanced computer vision systems to identify ripe produce and harvest them with precision, reducing waste and ensuring timely collection. The use of such technology not only addresses labor shortages but also enhances overall productivity.

Weed Control and Crop Monitoring

Weed management is another area where robotics is making significant strides. Autonomous weeding robots, like the **Blue River Technology's See & Spray**, employ machine learning algorithms to distinguish between crops and weeds. This targeted approach allows farmers to apply herbicides only where needed, reducing chemical use and promoting sustainable farming practices.

4.2 Robotics in Healthcare

Surgical Robots

In healthcare, robotic surgical systems have transformed surgical procedures by enhancing precision and reducing recovery times. The **da Vinci Surgical System** allows surgeons to perform minimally invasive surgeries with a level of dexterity that exceeds traditional techniques. For example, in prostatectomy procedures, the robotic system enables surgeons to remove cancerous tissue while preserving surrounding nerves and blood vessels, resulting in faster recovery and reduced complications.

Rehabilitation Robots

Robotic exoskeletons, such as the **EksoGT**, assist patients in regaining mobility after injuries or surgeries. These devices provide support and enable patients to practice walking, significantly improving their rehabilitation outcomes. Studies have shown that using robotic exoskeletons accelerates recovery times and enhances the overall effectiveness of physical therapy.

Telemedicine Robots

Telemedicine has gained prominence, especially in remote areas where access to healthcare is limited. Robots like **InTouch Health's telepresence robots** enable healthcare providers to conduct remote consultations, monitor patients, and provide care without being physically present. This technology ensures that patients receive timely medical attention, regardless of their location.

4.3 Robotics in Manufacturing

Industrial Automation

The manufacturing sector has long been a pioneer in adopting robotics for automation. Traditional industrial robots are employed for tasks such as welding, painting, and assembly, improving efficiency and accuracy. Companies like **Fanuc** and **KUKA** produce robotic arms that can perform repetitive tasks with high precision, resulting in reduced production times and lower labor costs.

Collaborative Robots (Cobots)

The introduction of collaborative robots has further enhanced manufacturing processes. Cobots are designed to work alongside human workers, assisting them in tasks that require precision and strength. For instance, the **UR Series by Universal Robots** features easy-to-program cobots that can handle various tasks, such as machine tending and packaging, while ensuring safety through built-in sensors and force-limiting technologies.

Quality Control Automation

Quality assurance is critical in manufacturing, and robotics plays a key role in this area. Automated inspection systems equipped with machine vision technology can detect defects in products with high accuracy. For example, **Cognex's vision systems** are widely used in manufacturing plants to ensure products meet quality standards, reducing the likelihood of defective items reaching consumers.

4.4 Benefits of Robotics in Agriculture, Healthcare, and Manufacturing

Increased Efficiency

Robotics significantly enhances efficiency in agriculture, healthcare, and manufacturing. Automated systems can operate continuously, performing tasks faster and with greater precision than human workers. This efficiency leads to higher output levels and reduced operational costs.

Improved Safety

In hazardous environments, such as manufacturing floors and agricultural fields, robots can perform dangerous tasks, reducing the risk of accidents and injuries to human workers. For instance, robots can handle heavy machinery, operate in extreme temperatures, and perform tasks in hazardous locations, enhancing workplace safety.

Data-Driven Decision Making

The integration of robotics with data analytics allows for better decision-making across industries. Robots equipped with sensors collect valuable data, providing insights that help improve processes and optimize resource use. In agriculture, this data enables farmers to make informed decisions about crop management, while in healthcare, it can inform treatment plans based on patient data.

4.5 Future Prospects

The future of robotics in agriculture, healthcare, and manufacturing is promising, with ongoing advancements in technology and increased investment in research and development. As artificial intelligence and machine learning continue to evolve, robots will become more autonomous and capable of handling complex tasks. The potential for robotics to revolutionize these sectors is immense, with applications ranging from automated farms to intelligent healthcare solutions that enhance patient care.

Conclusion

Robotics is transforming agriculture, healthcare, and manufacturing, driving efficiency, improving safety, and enabling innovative solutions to complex challenges. As technology continues to advance, the role of robotics in these sectors will only grow, shaping the future of work and enhancing the quality of life for individuals and communities.

5. Future Classifications and Innovations in Robotics

The field of robotics is continually evolving, driven by rapid advancements in technology and the increasing demand for automation across various sectors. As we look toward the future, it becomes essential to understand the classifications of robots that will likely emerge and the innovative technologies that will define the next generation of robotic systems. This chapter delves into potential future classifications of robots, highlights key innovations that are reshaping the industry, and explores the implications of these advancements for various applications.

5.1 Future Classifications of Robotics

5.1.1 Autonomous Robots

Autonomous robots, which can operate independently without human intervention, are expected to become more prevalent across different industries. These robots will utilize advanced artificial intelligence (AI) algorithms, enabling them to learn from their environments and make decisions based on real-time data. For example, **autonomous drones** used for surveillance or delivery can navigate complex environments, adapt to changing conditions, and optimize their routes based on traffic patterns.

5.1.2 Soft Robots

Soft robotics is an emerging field that focuses on creating robots from flexible materials that can mimic the movements and adaptability of biological organisms. Unlike traditional rigid robots, soft robots can navigate through confined spaces and handle delicate objects with ease. An example of this technology is the **Octopus-inspired soft robot**, which can grasp and manipulate fragile items, making it ideal for applications in fields such as agriculture and healthcare.

5.1.3 Swarm Robots

Swarm robotics draws inspiration from the collective behavior of social insects, such as ants and bees. These systems consist of multiple robots that work together to accomplish tasks efficiently. Future classifications may include autonomous swarm robots that can communicate and coordinate with one another to perform complex operations, such as environmental monitoring or search-and-rescue missions. An example of swarm robotics is the **Kilobots** project, where small robots collaborate to perform simple tasks like formation control and pattern generation.

5.1.4 Biohybrid Robots

Biohybrid robots combine biological components with synthetic systems to create more efficient and adaptable robotic solutions. This classification represents a fusion of living tissue and robotic technology, leading to innovations that can mimic biological functions. For example, researchers are developing **biohybrid robots** that utilize living muscle cells to generate movement, offering new possibilities for soft robotics and biomedical applications.

5.1.5 Exoskeletons and Augmented Robots

Exoskeletons are wearable robotic devices that enhance human capabilities by providing support and strength. The future of exoskeleton technology includes innovations that integrate AI and machine learning to adapt to users' movements and intentions. Augmented robots will work alongside humans, improving efficiency in sectors such as manufacturing and healthcare. The **EksoGT exoskeleton**, for instance, helps patients regain mobility during rehabilitation, showcasing the potential of exoskeletons in enhancing human performance.

5.2 Innovations in Robotics

5.2.1 Artificial Intelligence and Machine Learning

The integration of AI and machine learning is transforming robotics, enabling machines to learn from data and improve their performance over time. Future robots will incorporate sophisticated algorithms that allow them to adapt to changing environments and tasks. For instance, **robotic arms** used in manufacturing can learn from past assembly processes, optimizing their movements for increased efficiency.

5.2.2 Advanced Sensors and Perception

The development of advanced sensors is crucial for enhancing a robot's perception of its surroundings. Future robotics will likely employ sensors that can detect and interpret a wider range of stimuli, including touch, temperature, and even emotional cues. An example of this innovation is the use of **LiDAR** technology in autonomous vehicles, which enables them to create detailed 3D maps of their environment and navigate safely.

5.2.3 Human-Robot Interaction

Improving human-robot interaction is essential for the widespread adoption of robotic technologies. Future robots will be designed with intuitive interfaces that facilitate seamless communication and collaboration with humans. Innovations in natural language processing and emotion recognition will enable robots to understand and respond to human emotions, enhancing their usability in various applications. **Sophia**, a humanoid robot, exemplifies advancements in human-robot interaction, as it can engage in natural conversations and express emotions.

5.2.4 Energy Efficiency and Sustainability

As robotics becomes more integrated into our daily lives, energy efficiency and sustainability will be critical considerations for future developments. Innovations in energy storage, such as advanced batteries and energy harvesting technologies, will allow robots to operate for extended periods without frequent recharging. For instance, researchers are exploring **solar-powered robots** that can autonomously charge using sunlight, promoting sustainability in robotic applications.

5.2.5 Cloud Robotics

Cloud robotics leverages cloud computing to enable robots to share data and computational resources, enhancing their capabilities. Future robots will be able to access vast amounts of information and processing power from the cloud, allowing for real-time decision-making and improved performance. This approach will facilitate collaboration among robots and streamline their operations in various sectors, from logistics to healthcare.

5.3 Implications for Various Applications

The advancements and classifications of robotics will have far-reaching implications across various industries. In agriculture, robots will become integral in precision farming, enhancing crop yields while minimizing resource usage. In healthcare, innovative robotic systems will improve patient care and rehabilitation processes. Manufacturing will see increased automation, resulting in higher efficiency and product quality. As robots become more adaptable and capable of working alongside humans, the future of work will also change, necessitating a focus on upskilling and education for the workforce.

Conclusion

The future of robotics promises exciting innovations and new classifications that will reshape industries and enhance our daily lives. As technology continues to advance, the potential applications of robotics will expand, presenting opportunities and challenges that must be addressed. By understanding the emerging classifications and innovations in robotics, we can better prepare for a future where robots play an integral role in society.

Chapter 3: Technologies Behind Robotics

1. Key Components of Robotic Systems (Sensors, Actuators, etc.)
2. Advances in Artificial Intelligence and Machine Learning for Robotics
3. Control Systems and Robotics Programming
4. Human-Robot Interaction Technologies
5. Future Technological Innovations and Their Potential Impact

Chapter 3

Technologies Behind Robotics

Introduction

As robotics continues to evolve, the underlying technologies that power robotic systems play a crucial role in determining their capabilities and applications. This chapter explores the key components of robotic systems, including sensors, actuators, and control systems, which serve as the foundation for creating intelligent and versatile robots. Additionally, we will delve into the advancements in artificial intelligence (AI) and machine learning that enable robots to learn from their environments and improve their performance over time.

Understanding human-robot interaction technologies is also essential, as these systems facilitate seamless communication and collaboration between humans and robots. The chapter will conclude with a discussion on future technological innovations that promise to enhance the functionality and efficiency of robotic systems, as well as their potential impact across various industries.

Through a comprehensive exploration of these technologies, we aim to provide readers with a deeper understanding of the mechanisms that drive robotics, the advancements that are shaping the future of the field, and the implications for various applications in everyday life. As we navigate through the complexities of robotics technology, it becomes evident that the integration of these components not only defines the capabilities of robots but also paves the way for new possibilities in automation and intelligent systems.

1. Key Components of Robotic Systems (Sensors, Actuators, etc.)

Robotic systems are complex entities composed of various components that work in harmony to perform specific tasks. Among these components, sensors and actuators play critical roles, serving as the sensory and motor systems of robots, respectively. Understanding these key components is essential for grasping how robots interact with their environments and carry out functions ranging from simple movements to complex operations in dynamic settings.

This chapter will explore the main components of robotic systems in detail, focusing on sensors and actuators, as well as other essential elements that contribute to the functionality and performance of robots. By examining the principles, applications, and advancements in these components, we aim to provide insights into the design and development of robotic systems.

1.1 Sensors in Robotics

Sensors are devices that enable robots to perceive their environment. They gather information about physical properties such as distance, temperature, pressure, and light, allowing robots to make informed decisions based on their surroundings. The effectiveness of a robot in performing its tasks largely depends on the quality and type of sensors it employs.

1.1.1 Types of Sensors

- **Proximity Sensors**: These sensors detect the presence or absence of an object within a certain range without making physical contact. Common examples include infrared sensors and ultrasonic sensors, which are widely used in robotic applications to avoid obstacles.

- **Vision Sensors**: Cameras and visual sensors capture images and videos, allowing robots to process visual information. Machine vision systems are used in quality control in manufacturing, enabling robots to identify defects in products.

- **Lidar Sensors**: Light Detection and Ranging (Lidar) sensors emit laser beams to measure distances by calculating the time it takes for the light to return. Lidar is commonly used in autonomous vehicles for mapping and navigation.

- **Tactile Sensors**: These sensors provide feedback on touch and pressure. Tactile sensors are essential in robotic grippers, allowing robots to handle delicate objects without causing damage.

- **Inertial Sensors**: These include accelerometers and gyroscopes, which measure the orientation and movement of the robot. Inertial sensors are crucial for stabilizing robots and ensuring accurate navigation.

1.2 Actuators in Robotics

Actuators are the components responsible for converting electrical energy into mechanical motion. They enable robots to move and interact with their environment by performing tasks such as lifting, rotating, or manipulating objects.

1.2.1 Types of Actuators

- **Electric Motors**: These are the most common type of actuators used in robotics. They convert electrical energy into rotational motion, allowing robots to move joints and limbs. Different types of electric motors, such as DC motors and stepper motors, are selected based on the specific application requirements.

- **Hydraulic Actuators**: These actuators use pressurized fluid to produce motion. Hydraulic systems are capable of generating high forces, making them suitable for heavy-duty applications such as construction robots and industrial machinery.

- **Pneumatic Actuators**: Pneumatic actuators utilize compressed air to create motion. They are lightweight and provide rapid response times, making them ideal for applications that require quick movements, such as pick-and-place robots.

- **Servo Motors**: These are specialized electric motors that provide precise control of angular position. Servo motors are widely used in robotic arms for tasks requiring high precision and repeatability, such as assembly operations.

1.3 Other Key Components

In addition to sensors and actuators, several other components are critical to the functioning of robotic systems.

- **Control Systems**: Control systems manage the operation of robots by processing input from sensors and sending commands to actuators. They can be classified into open-loop and closed-loop control systems. Closed-loop systems use feedback from sensors to adjust the robot's actions in real time.

- **Power Supply**: Robots require a reliable power source to operate their sensors and actuators. This may include batteries, solar panels, or external power supplies, depending on the robot's design and application.

- **Computational Unit**: The computational unit, often a microcontroller or computer, processes data from sensors and executes algorithms to control the robot's behavior. Advanced robots may use onboard computers with AI capabilities to enable complex decision-making.

- **Communication Interfaces**: Communication interfaces enable robots to exchange information with other devices and systems. This includes wireless communication technologies like Wi-Fi, Bluetooth, and Zigbee, which facilitate remote control and data sharing.

1.4 Examples of Robotic Systems

To illustrate the application of sensors and actuators in robotic systems, consider the following examples:

- **Industrial Robots**: In manufacturing environments, industrial robots utilize a combination of sensors for object detection and actuators for precise movements. For instance, a robotic arm in an assembly line may use vision sensors to identify parts and servo motors to position them accurately.

- **Autonomous Vehicles**: Autonomous cars rely heavily on Lidar sensors for mapping their environment and electric motors for propulsion. These vehicles integrate various sensors to perceive obstacles and make driving decisions based on real-time data.

- **Medical Robots**: Surgical robots, such as the da Vinci Surgical System, employ advanced sensors for visual feedback and precise actuators to perform delicate surgical procedures. These systems enhance the surgeon's capabilities and improve patient outcomes.

Conclusion

Understanding the key components of robotic systems is essential for grasping how these machines operate and interact with their environments. Sensors provide critical information, while actuators enable movement and interaction. Together with control systems and computational units, these components create the foundation for advanced robotics applications across various industries. As technology continues to advance, the integration of these components will lead to more capable, intelligent, and versatile robotic systems.

2. Advances in Artificial Intelligence and Machine Learning for Robotics

Artificial Intelligence (AI) and Machine Learning (ML) are at the forefront of transforming robotics, enabling machines to perform complex tasks with increasing levels of autonomy, efficiency, and intelligence. Over the last few decades, significant advancements in AI and ML have led to the development of more capable robotic systems that can perceive, reason, and interact with their environment in ways previously thought impossible.

This chapter explores the integration of AI and ML in robotics, focusing on the underlying technologies, methodologies, and their applications. We will delve into various AI techniques used in robotics, the role of data in machine learning, and real-world examples of robots powered by these technologies. Furthermore, we will discuss the challenges faced in implementing AI and ML in robotic systems and the future prospects of these advancements in the field of robotics.

2.1 Understanding Artificial Intelligence in Robotics

Artificial Intelligence refers to the simulation of human intelligence processes by machines, particularly computer systems. In the context of robotics, AI enables robots to analyze data, learn from experiences, and make decisions based on that information. The key aspects of AI relevant to robotics include:

- **Perception**: This involves enabling robots to perceive their environment using sensors and interpret the data collected. AI algorithms, particularly those in computer vision and natural language processing, play a vital role in enabling robots to understand visual and auditory information.

- **Reasoning**: AI systems can process information and draw conclusions based on a set of rules or learned data. In robotics, this is essential for tasks like navigation, planning, and decision-making.

- **Learning**: Through machine learning, robots can improve their performance over time by learning from past experiences. This ability to learn from data allows robots to adapt to changing environments and tasks.

2.2 Machine Learning Techniques in Robotics

Machine Learning is a subset of AI that focuses on the development of algorithms that allow computers to learn from and make predictions based on data. Several machine learning techniques are particularly relevant to robotics:

- **Supervised Learning**: This approach involves training a model on a labeled dataset, where the correct output is provided for each input. For example, robots can be trained to identify objects by providing them with images and corresponding labels, enabling them to recognize similar objects in real-world scenarios.

- **Unsupervised Learning**: In this case, the model is trained on an unlabeled dataset and must find patterns or groupings on its own. This technique can be useful for robots that need to categorize data without prior knowledge, such as clustering similar types of objects or behaviors.

- **Reinforcement Learning**: This approach involves training agents to make decisions by rewarding them for desirable actions and penalizing them for undesirable ones. Robots can learn complex tasks, such as navigating through a maze, by exploring different paths and receiving feedback on their performance.

- **Deep Learning**: A subset of machine learning that utilizes neural networks with many layers, deep learning has shown remarkable success in areas like computer vision and speech recognition. Robots use deep learning to process large amounts of visual data, enabling them to identify and interact with objects more effectively.

2.3 Real-World Applications of AI and ML in Robotics

The integration of AI and ML has led to the emergence of various innovative robotic applications across different sectors. Here are some notable examples:

- **Autonomous Vehicles**: Companies like Waymo and Tesla are leveraging AI and machine learning to develop self-driving cars. These vehicles utilize deep learning algorithms to process data from sensors, make real-time decisions, and navigate complex environments.

- **Industrial Robotics**: In manufacturing, robots equipped with AI and ML can optimize production processes, perform quality control, and adapt to changing production lines. For example, FANUC's robots use machine learning to improve their performance over time, enabling them to handle a wider variety of tasks with greater precision.

- **Healthcare Robots**: Robots like the da Vinci Surgical System utilize AI algorithms to assist surgeons in performing minimally invasive surgeries. These systems learn from past surgeries to enhance their precision and adaptability, significantly improving patient outcomes.

- **Service Robots**: In the hospitality industry, robots such as Relay and JEEVES use AI to navigate and interact with guests. These robots learn from their experiences, enabling them to provide better service and respond to customer inquiries more effectively.

2.4 Challenges in Implementing AI and ML in Robotics

Despite the advancements in AI and ML, several challenges persist in their implementation within robotic systems:

- **Data Quality and Quantity**: High-quality, labeled datasets are crucial for training machine learning models. However, collecting sufficient data can be difficult, particularly in dynamic environments where robots operate.

- **Real-Time Processing**: Many robotic applications require real-time decision-making capabilities. Achieving low-latency processing while maintaining high accuracy in AI algorithms is a significant technical challenge.

- **Safety and Reliability**: Ensuring the safety and reliability of AI-powered robots is paramount, especially in applications where human lives are at stake, such as healthcare and autonomous driving.

- **Ethical Considerations**: As robots become more autonomous, ethical concerns regarding their decision-making processes, data privacy, and potential job displacement arise. Addressing these concerns is essential for fostering public trust in robotics.

2.5 Future Prospects of AI and ML in Robotics

The future of robotics will increasingly rely on the continuous advancements in AI and machine learning. Some anticipated trends include:

- **Improved Human-Robot Collaboration**: As robots become more intelligent and capable, they will work more effectively alongside humans in various environments, enhancing productivity and efficiency.

- **Enhanced Adaptability**: Future robots will possess advanced learning capabilities, allowing them to adapt to new tasks and environments autonomously without extensive retraining.

- **Integration of AI and IoT**: The convergence of AI with the Internet of Things (IoT) will enable robots to leverage vast amounts of data from connected devices, leading to smarter decision-making and improved operational efficiency.

- **Emphasis on Explainability**: As robots become more autonomous, the need for explainable AI will grow. Ensuring that robots can communicate their decision-making processes transparently will be essential for building trust and accountability.

Conclusion

The integration of artificial intelligence and machine learning in robotics has transformed the landscape of this field, enabling the development of sophisticated and capable robotic systems. By understanding the fundamental concepts and advancements in AI and ML, we can better appreciate their impact on various applications and the future of robotics. As technology continues to evolve, the potential for AI-powered robots to enhance our lives and industries remains immense.

3. Control Systems and Robotics Programming

Control systems and programming form the backbone of robotics technology, enabling robots to perform tasks accurately and efficiently. Control systems are crucial for managing the behavior of robotic systems, while programming provides the instructions that dictate how robots interact with their environment. This chapter delves into the principles of control systems, the programming languages and paradigms used in robotics, and the significance of simulation and real-time systems in robot development.

As robotics technology continues to advance, understanding control systems and programming techniques is essential for developing more autonomous, intelligent, and versatile robots. We will explore the various types of control systems, the role of programming in robotic applications, and the emerging trends that are shaping the future of robotics programming.

3.1 Understanding Control Systems in Robotics

Control systems are designed to manage the behavior of dynamic systems by adjusting their inputs based on feedback from their outputs. In robotics, control systems play a vital role in ensuring that robots perform tasks accurately and respond appropriately to changes in their environment. Control systems can be broadly classified into two categories: open-loop and closed-loop systems.

3.1.1 Open-Loop Control Systems

Open-loop control systems operate without feedback; they provide an input to the system based solely on predetermined instructions. An example of an open-loop control system in robotics is a simple conveyor belt that moves materials at a constant speed. The system operates based on the input it receives, but it does not adjust its operation based on the actual output or conditions of the material being transported.

3.1.2 Closed-Loop Control Systems

Closed-loop control systems, also known as feedback control systems, utilize feedback from the system's output to adjust the input accordingly. This type of system is crucial in robotics, as it allows robots to respond to changes in their environment and maintain desired performance levels. For instance, a robotic arm equipped with sensors can monitor its position and adjust its movements to ensure that it accurately picks up an object, even if the object's position varies.

3.2 Control System Architectures

Various control system architectures can be employed in robotics, depending on the complexity and requirements of the robotic application:

3.2.1 Proportional-Integral-Derivative (PID) Control

PID control is a widely used control strategy in robotics that combines three components: proportional, integral, and derivative. This approach allows for precise control of dynamic systems by minimizing the error between the desired and actual output. For example, a robotic arm's position can be controlled using a PID controller to ensure accurate positioning and smooth motion.

3.2.2 Model Predictive Control (MPC)

Model Predictive Control is an advanced control strategy that uses a dynamic model of the system to predict future behavior and optimize control actions accordingly. MPC is particularly useful in robotics for applications that require handling constraints and managing multi-variable systems. For example, self-driving cars use MPC to plan safe trajectories while considering the dynamics of the vehicle and the surrounding environment.

3.3 Robotics Programming Languages

Programming plays a critical role in robotics, as it defines the logic and instructions that guide robotic behavior. Several programming languages and frameworks are commonly used in the robotics field:

3.3.1 Robot Operating System (ROS)

ROS is an open-source framework widely adopted in robotics for developing complex robotic systems. It provides libraries and tools for robot software development, enabling modular programming and seamless communication between different components. ROS supports various programming languages, including

C++ and Python, allowing developers to choose the language that best suits their needs.

3.3.2 C and C++

C and C++ are popular programming languages in robotics due to their efficiency and low-level hardware control capabilities. These languages are commonly used for developing real-time control systems and performance-critical applications, such as embedded systems in robots.

3.3.3 Python

Python is increasingly being used in robotics due to its simplicity and ease of use. It is particularly favored for high-level programming, rapid prototyping, and integrating machine learning algorithms into robotic applications. The availability of libraries like NumPy and OpenCV further enhances Python's utility in robotics.

3.4 Robotics Simulation

Simulation is an essential aspect of robotics development, allowing engineers and researchers to model and test robotic systems in virtual environments before deploying them in the real world. Simulation tools enable the testing of control algorithms, programming logic, and the overall performance of robotic systems without the risk of damaging physical components.

3.4.1 Gazebo

Gazebo is a popular open-source robotics simulator that provides a realistic environment for testing robotic systems. It allows developers to simulate sensor data, physical interactions, and complex environments, making it an invaluable tool for validating control algorithms and programming logic.

3.4.2 V-REP (CoppeliaSim)

V-REP, now known as CoppeliaSim, is another widely used robotics simulation platform that supports various robot models and control methods. It provides a comprehensive environment for developing and testing robotic applications, allowing users to create complex simulations with minimal programming.

3.5 Real-Time Systems in Robotics

Real-time systems are crucial for robotics applications that require timely responses to dynamic conditions. In real-time systems, the correctness of an operation depends not only on the logical result but also on the time at which the results are produced.

3.5.1 Real-Time Operating Systems (RTOS)

Real-Time Operating Systems (RTOS) are designed to manage hardware resources and ensure that critical tasks are completed within defined time constraints. RTOS is essential for applications like industrial robots and autonomous vehicles, where delays in response can lead to safety risks or operational failures.

3.5.2 Scheduling Algorithms

Scheduling algorithms play a key role in real-time systems by determining the order in which tasks are executed. In robotics, efficient scheduling ensures that critical tasks receive the necessary processing time, allowing the robot to respond promptly to external stimuli.

Conclusion

Control systems and programming are foundational elements of robotic technology, enabling robots to function autonomously and effectively. Understanding the principles of control systems, the various programming languages and frameworks, and the importance of simulation and real-time systems is essential for developing advanced robotic applications. As robotics technology continues to evolve, these concepts will remain critical in shaping the future of robotics, allowing for more intelligent, capable, and versatile systems.

4. Human-Robot Interaction Technologies

The relationship between humans and robots is becoming increasingly important as robotics technology continues to advance. Human-robot interaction (HRI) refers to the interdisciplinary study of how humans and robots communicate, collaborate, and coexist in various environments. As robots are deployed in more complex and sensitive roles—ranging from healthcare assistants to autonomous vehicles—the need for effective interaction mechanisms is paramount.

This chapter explores the technologies that underpin human-robot interaction, focusing on advancements that enhance communication, collaboration, and emotional engagement between humans and robots. We will delve into various interaction modalities, including natural language processing, gesture recognition, and emotional intelligence, and examine how these technologies are shaping the future of HRI.

4.1 Natural Language Processing (NLP)

Natural language processing is a key technology that enables robots to understand and respond to human speech. Advances in NLP are making it possible for robots to engage in more natural and fluid conversations with users.

4.1.1 Speech Recognition

The ability of robots to recognize and interpret spoken language is fundamental to effective communication. Technologies like automatic speech recognition (ASR) allow robots to convert spoken words into text, facilitating interaction. For example, voice-activated home assistants, such as Amazon Alexa and Google Home, utilize ASR to understand user commands, enabling them to control smart devices and provide information.

4.1.2 Dialogue Management

Beyond mere speech recognition, robots must also manage conversations effectively. Dialogue management systems enable robots to maintain context, understand user intent, and respond appropriately. For instance, customer service robots can engage users in multi-turn dialogues, addressing queries and resolving issues in a coherent manner.

4.2 Gesture Recognition

Gesture recognition technology allows robots to interpret human body language and gestures, enhancing non-verbal communication.

4.2.1 Vision-Based Gesture Recognition

Robots equipped with cameras and computer vision algorithms can analyze human gestures in real-time. This capability is particularly useful in collaborative environments, where robots need to understand human cues. For example, manufacturing robots can detect hand signals from human workers to initiate or halt operations, ensuring safety and efficiency.

4.2.2 Touch and Haptic Feedback

Haptic feedback technology provides tactile sensations that allow robots to convey information through touch. For instance, a robotic arm may use haptic feedback to communicate its position and force applied during a collaborative task. This interaction modality enhances the user experience and fosters a more intuitive collaboration between humans and robots.

4.3 Emotional Intelligence in Robots

Integrating emotional intelligence into robots enables them to recognize and respond to human emotions, fostering empathetic interactions.

4.3.1 Emotion Recognition

Robots can utilize facial recognition and voice analysis to gauge human emotions. By understanding emotional states, robots can adapt their responses accordingly. For example, a social robot in a healthcare setting may detect when a patient is feeling anxious and respond with calming language or behaviors.

4.3.2 Adaptive Behavior

Emotional intelligence also allows robots to exhibit adaptive behavior based on human emotions. For instance, companion robots can adjust their tone of voice, body language, and actions to align with the emotional needs of users, creating a more engaging and supportive interaction.

4.4 Collaborative Robots (Cobots)

Collaborative robots, or cobots, are designed to work alongside humans in shared spaces. The interaction technologies in cobots play a crucial role in ensuring safe and efficient collaboration.

4.4.1 Safety Features

Safety is a primary concern in human-robot collaboration. Advanced sensors and machine learning algorithms enable cobots to detect human presence and react accordingly. For example, a cobot working in a manufacturing environment can slow down or stop its operation when a human worker approaches, minimizing the risk of accidents.

4.4.2 Communication and Coordination

Effective communication between cobots and human workers is vital for seamless collaboration. Cobots may use visual displays, auditory signals, or even physical gestures to convey information to their human counterparts. This capability ensures that both parties can coordinate their actions and complete tasks efficiently.

4.5 Future Directions in Human-Robot Interaction

As robotics technology continues to evolve, the field of human-robot interaction is expected to advance significantly. Future trends may include:

4.5.1 Enhanced Multimodal Interactions

Future robots will likely employ multimodal interaction strategies, combining speech, gesture, and emotional recognition to create more holistic communication experiences. This advancement will improve the intuitiveness of human-robot interactions and make robots more effective in various applications.

4.5.2 Personalized Interaction Experiences

Robots equipped with machine learning algorithms may learn individual user preferences over time, allowing them to customize interactions based on past behaviors and interactions. This personalization will enhance user satisfaction and engagement.

Conclusion

Human-robot interaction technologies are central to the effective integration of robots into daily life. By leveraging advancements in natural language processing, gesture recognition, and emotional intelligence, robots can communicate and collaborate more effectively with humans. As these technologies continue to develop, they will pave the way for more sophisticated and empathetic human-robot relationships, ultimately enhancing the utility and acceptance of robots in various sectors.

5. Future Technological Innovations and Their Potential Impact

The field of robotics is on the cusp of transformative change, fueled by rapid advancements in technology and an increasing demand for automation across various sectors. As we look toward the future, several key technological innovations are poised to reshape the landscape of robotics. These innovations promise to enhance the capabilities of robots, improve human-robot interaction, and expand the range of applications in which robots can be effectively deployed.

This chapter explores the emerging technologies that are likely to influence the future of robotics. By examining advancements in artificial intelligence (AI), machine learning (ML), sensor technologies, and materials science, we can gain insights into the potential impact of these innovations on the robotics industry and society as a whole. Additionally, we will discuss the ethical considerations and challenges that may arise with the adoption of these technologies.

5.1 Advancements in Artificial Intelligence and Machine Learning

Artificial intelligence and machine learning are at the forefront of robotics innovation. The integration of AI into robotic systems enables them to perform complex tasks, learn from their environment, and adapt to changing conditions.

5.1.1 Enhanced Decision-Making Capabilities

Future robots will leverage advanced AI algorithms to improve their decision-making capabilities. This means robots will not only execute predefined tasks but also analyze data in real-time to make informed decisions. For example, autonomous vehicles will rely on AI to interpret sensor data, navigate dynamic environments, and avoid obstacles. This ability to make split-second decisions will significantly enhance safety and efficiency in transportation.

5.1.2 Personalized Interactions

Machine learning algorithms will enable robots to understand and respond to individual user preferences and behaviors. For instance, companion robots in healthcare settings may learn a patient's routines and emotional responses, allowing them to provide tailored support and companionship. This level of personalization will improve the effectiveness of robotic assistants and foster stronger human-robot relationships.

5.2 Advances in Sensor Technologies

Sensors are critical components of robotic systems, providing the necessary data for navigation, interaction, and operation. Future innovations in sensor technologies will enhance robots' perception and capabilities.

5.2.1 Multi-Modal Sensors

The development of multi-modal sensors—devices that integrate multiple types of sensing modalities—will allow robots to perceive their environment more comprehensively. For instance, combining visual, auditory, and tactile sensors will enable robots to understand complex scenarios better. In domestic environments, a multi-modal robot could recognize when a person is speaking, respond appropriately, and even detect if someone is in distress based on visual and auditory cues.

5.2.2 Advanced Environmental Sensors

Future robots will utilize advanced environmental sensors, such as LiDAR (Light Detection and Ranging) and ultrasonic sensors, to create detailed maps of their surroundings. These technologies will enhance navigation capabilities, allowing robots to maneuver through complex environments with greater precision. For example, autonomous delivery drones will rely on environmental sensors to navigate urban landscapes safely and efficiently.

5.3 Innovative Materials and Manufacturing Techniques

The future of robotics will also be shaped by advancements in materials science and manufacturing techniques. Innovations in these areas will enable the development of more capable, flexible, and resilient robots.

5.3.1 Soft Robotics

Soft robotics is an emerging field that focuses on creating robots from flexible materials that can mimic biological organisms. These robots are designed to be more adaptable and safe for interaction with humans. For example, soft robotic grippers can handle delicate objects without causing damage, making them ideal for applications in food handling or healthcare.

5.3.2 3D Printing and Customization

The adoption of 3D printing technology in robotics manufacturing will enable rapid prototyping and customization of robotic components. This flexibility will allow developers to create tailored robots for specific applications, reducing development time and costs. For instance, customized robotic arms can be designed for unique tasks in manufacturing, optimizing productivity and efficiency.

5.4 Collaborative Robots and Human-Robot Teams

As robots become more advanced, their ability to collaborate with humans will improve, leading to the rise of human-robot teams in various sectors.

5.4.1 Enhanced Collaboration

Future collaborative robots, or cobots, will be designed to work alongside humans in shared environments. These robots will possess advanced sensing and communication capabilities, allowing them to understand human intentions and respond appropriately. In manufacturing, cobots may assist workers by lifting heavy objects or performing repetitive tasks, thereby improving productivity while reducing the risk of injury.

5.4.2 Multi-Robot Systems

The future will also see the emergence of multi-robot systems, where several robots work together to accomplish complex tasks. These systems will rely on sophisticated algorithms for coordination and communication. For example, swarms of drones could be deployed for agricultural monitoring, collaborating to gather data and optimize crop management practices.

5.5 Ethical Considerations and Challenges

With the rise of advanced robotics technologies, ethical considerations and challenges will become increasingly important.

5.5.1 Job Displacement and Workforce Impact

As robots become more capable and widespread, there is growing concern about job displacement in various industries. While automation can improve efficiency and reduce costs, it may also lead to significant changes in the workforce. Policymakers and industry leaders must address these challenges by developing strategies to reskill workers and ensure a smooth transition to an automated economy.

5.5.2 Privacy and Security Concerns

The integration of robots into everyday life raises important privacy and security concerns. Robots equipped with sensors may collect sensitive data about individuals and their environments. Ensuring that this data is handled responsibly and ethically will be crucial in maintaining public trust in robotic technologies.

Conclusion

The future of robotics is poised for unprecedented advancements driven by innovations in artificial intelligence, sensor technologies, materials science, and collaboration methods. These technological innovations have the potential to transform industries, enhance human-robot interaction, and improve the quality of life for individuals. However, alongside these opportunities, ethical considerations must be addressed to ensure that the deployment of robotics benefits society as a whole. As we navigate this exciting landscape, continuous research and dialogue will be essential in shaping a future where robots and humans coexist harmoniously.

Chapter 4: Design and Development of Robotics

1. Principles of Robotic Design for Efficiency and Performance
2. Software Development for Robotic Applications
3. Prototyping and Testing in Robotics Development
4. Design Considerations for Safety and Usability
5. Innovations in Materials and Manufacturing Techniques for Robots

Chapter 4

Design and Development of Robotics

Introduction

The design and development of robotic systems is a complex and interdisciplinary process that integrates principles from engineering, computer science, and user experience design. As the demand for robots across various sectors continues to rise, understanding the foundational aspects of their design becomes increasingly critical. This chapter delves into the essential principles, methodologies, and innovations that shape the field of robotics design and development.

At the heart of effective robotic design lies the need for efficiency and performance. This involves not only the mechanical and electronic components but also the software that drives the robot's functionalities. The principles of robotic design must account for various factors, including the robot's intended application, operating environment, and user interaction.

Software development plays a crucial role in robotics, providing the necessary algorithms and systems that enable robots to perform tasks autonomously or in collaboration with humans. As robots become more sophisticated, the software must evolve to support advanced functionalities, including machine learning and artificial intelligence, allowing for smarter and more adaptable robotic systems.

Prototyping and testing are integral to the robotics development process. Iterative design practices enable engineers and designers to refine their concepts, identify potential issues, and ensure that the final product meets the required performance and safety standards. Rigorous testing not only verifies functionality but also assesses the robot's reliability and effectiveness in real-world scenarios.

Safety and usability considerations are paramount in robotic design, especially as robots are increasingly integrated into everyday environments where they interact with humans. Ensuring that robots operate safely while being user-friendly enhances their acceptance and effectiveness. Design strategies must incorporate safety features and intuitive interfaces that cater to a wide range of users.

Lastly, innovations in materials and manufacturing techniques are revolutionizing robotics development. The advent of lightweight, durable materials, along with advancements in 3D printing and other manufacturing technologies, allows for the creation of robots that are not only efficient but also cost-effective and scalable.

In summary, this chapter will explore these critical aspects of robotics design and development, providing insights into the principles that guide the creation of efficient, safe, and high-performance robotic systems. As we navigate through these topics, we will uncover the challenges and opportunities that lie ahead in the ever-evolving field of robotics.

1. Principles of Robotic Design for Efficiency and Performance

The design of robotic systems is a multifaceted endeavor that directly influences their efficiency and performance. As robots are increasingly utilized in diverse applications, from manufacturing to healthcare, the principles underlying their design become pivotal. This section explores the key principles that guide robotic design, emphasizing efficiency, performance, and user interaction. We will delve into the various aspects of robotic design, supported by relevant examples that illustrate these principles in action.

1.1 Understanding Efficiency in Robotics

Efficiency in robotics refers to the optimal use of resources—be it energy, time, or materials—while achieving desired outcomes. A well-designed robot minimizes waste, enhances productivity, and operates seamlessly within its environment. Key factors influencing robotic efficiency include:

- **Energy Consumption**: Efficient robots are designed to consume minimal energy while performing tasks. For instance, robotic arms used in manufacturing employ servo motors that adjust their power usage based on load conditions, conserving energy during idle times.

- **Task Optimization**: Robots should be capable of executing tasks in the least amount of time possible. For example, in logistics, autonomous mobile robots (AMRs) are programmed to optimize their routes to reduce travel time between pick-up and drop-off points, thus enhancing overall productivity.

- **Material Efficiency**: The selection of materials impacts not only the robot's weight but also its operational efficiency. Lightweight materials, such as carbon fiber or aluminum alloys, are often used in robotic design to reduce mass, thereby improving speed and energy efficiency.

1.2 Performance Metrics in Robotic Design

Performance metrics provide quantifiable standards against which the efficiency of a robot can be measured. Key performance indicators (KPIs) include:

- **Speed**: The rate at which a robot completes a task is a primary performance metric. For example, in automotive assembly lines, robots that can weld parts together in fractions of a second significantly reduce production time.

- **Accuracy**: Precision is critical in tasks such as surgical robotics, where the slightest deviation can have serious consequences. Robots like the da Vinci Surgical System utilize advanced vision systems and feedback loops to achieve remarkable accuracy in delicate procedures.

- **Reliability**: A reliable robot consistently performs its tasks without failure. Designing for reliability involves selecting durable components and conducting extensive testing. Industrial robots, like those from FANUC, are designed to operate continuously with minimal downtime, ensuring high productivity in factories.

1.3 The Role of Ergonomics in Robotic Design

Ergonomics, or human factors engineering, is integral to robotic design, particularly in applications involving human-robot collaboration. Robots must be designed with user interaction in mind, ensuring that they are intuitive and safe for human operators. Key ergonomic considerations include:

- **User Interface Design**: An effective user interface simplifies operation and enhances user experience. For instance, collaborative robots (cobots) often feature touchscreens and easy-to-understand controls that allow operators to program tasks quickly.

- **Safety Features**: Safety is paramount in environments where humans and robots interact. Robots equipped with sensors to detect human presence, such as those used in warehouses, can halt operation if a person enters their work zone, preventing accidents.

- **Training and Support**: Providing adequate training for operators is crucial. User manuals, training sessions, and support systems should be developed to ensure that users can effectively engage with robotic systems.

1.4 Scalability and Modularity in Design

Scalability and modularity are essential principles that facilitate the adaptability of robotic systems to different tasks and environments.

- **Modular Design**: Robots designed with interchangeable components can easily adapt to various applications. For example, modular robotic kits used in education allow students to build and customize robots for different tasks, enhancing their learning experience.

- **Scalable Solutions**: As demand fluctuates, scalable robotic systems can be expanded or reduced in capacity. For instance, manufacturing plants often use flexible robotic systems that can be reconfigured to produce different products based on market needs.

1.5 Real-World Examples of Efficient Robotic Design

Several real-world examples illustrate the principles of efficient robotic design:

- **Boston Dynamics' Spot**: This quadrupedal robot exemplifies efficiency through its ability to navigate diverse terrains while maintaining balance and stability. Its design allows it to perform tasks in various environments, from construction sites to disaster zones.

- **KUKA's LBR iiwa**: This lightweight collaborative robot is designed with sensitivity and flexibility in mind. It can work alongside humans safely, making it ideal for assembly tasks in industries where precision and adaptability are critical.

- **RoboCup Soccer**: The annual RoboCup competition showcases the principles of robotic design in a competitive environment. Teams design robots that must operate efficiently, coordinate with one another, and adapt to dynamic conditions on the field, highlighting the importance of performance metrics.

Conclusion

In conclusion, the principles of robotic design for efficiency and performance encompass a wide range of factors, from energy consumption to user ergonomics. As robotics technology continues to evolve, these principles will guide the development of more sophisticated systems capable of addressing complex challenges across various industries. By prioritizing efficiency, performance, and user interaction, designers can create robots that not only enhance productivity but also foster positive human-robot collaboration.

2. Software Development for Robotic Applications

Software development is a crucial aspect of robotics, enabling machines to perform complex tasks autonomously and interact with their environments and human operators. The software provides the intelligence behind robotic systems, allowing them to process sensory information, make decisions, and execute actions. This section will explore the various facets of software development in robotics, including programming languages, frameworks, and methodologies. We will examine real-world examples to illustrate the concepts discussed and provide a comprehensive understanding of how software drives robotic functionality.

2.1 The Role of Software in Robotics

Software in robotics encompasses a wide range of functions, including:

- **Control Algorithms**: These algorithms determine how a robot reacts to its environment, controlling its movements and actions based on input from sensors. For example, a self-driving car uses complex control algorithms to navigate roads safely.

- **Sensor Integration**: Robots rely on sensors to perceive their surroundings. Software integrates data from these sensors, allowing robots to make informed decisions. For instance, robotic vacuum cleaners use sensor data to map their environment and avoid obstacles.

- **Data Processing**: Robots often process large amounts of data in real-time. Advanced software frameworks, such as Robot Operating System (ROS), enable efficient data handling, allowing robots to analyze sensor input and adapt their behavior accordingly.

2.2 Programming Languages for Robotics

Various programming languages are used in robotics, each serving different purposes based on the specific requirements of a project. Some of the most common languages include:

- **C++**: Known for its efficiency and control over system resources, C++ is widely used in robotics for developing performance-critical applications. For example, many robotic systems in the automotive industry are programmed in C++ to ensure real-time responsiveness.

- **Python**: Python's simplicity and extensive libraries make it popular for rapid prototyping and development in robotics. Its ease of use allows developers to quickly implement algorithms and test them. For instance, ROS provides Python bindings, enabling developers to create robotic applications with less code.

- **MATLAB**: Often used in academic settings, MATLAB is favored for its robust mathematical capabilities and toolboxes specifically designed for robotics. Researchers frequently use MATLAB for simulation and control design, particularly in educational robotics projects.

2.3 Software Development Methodologies

Software development methodologies play a significant role in the robotics software lifecycle, influencing how projects are planned, developed, and maintained. Common methodologies include:

- **Agile Development**: Agile emphasizes iterative development and collaboration, making it well-suited for robotics projects where requirements may change frequently. This approach allows teams to adapt to new challenges and incorporate feedback rapidly.

- **Model-Based Development**: This methodology uses models to represent the behavior and design of robotic systems. Tools like Simulink allow developers to simulate and analyze system performance before implementing them in hardware.

- **Continuous Integration/Continuous Deployment (CI/CD)**: In robotics, CI/CD practices help automate the testing and deployment of software, ensuring that updates can be rolled out quickly and reliably. For example, the software for autonomous drones often employs CI/CD to keep their algorithms up-to-date with the latest improvements.

2.4 Software Frameworks and Tools

Robotics development is facilitated by various software frameworks and tools that streamline the process and provide essential functionality. Notable frameworks include:

- **Robot Operating System (ROS)**: ROS is a flexible framework that provides libraries and tools for building robotic applications. It simplifies the process of integrating sensors, actuators, and algorithms, enabling developers to focus on high-level functionality rather than low-level hardware interfacing. For instance, many robotic research projects leverage ROS for developing autonomous navigation systems.

- **Gazebo**: Gazebo is a powerful simulation tool that works with ROS, allowing developers to test and visualize their robotic applications in a virtual environment. This enables them to evaluate performance and troubleshoot issues before deploying the software on actual robots.

- **OpenCV**: OpenCV is an open-source computer vision library widely used in robotics for image processing and analysis. Robots equipped with vision systems utilize OpenCV for tasks such as object detection and recognition, enabling them to interact with their environment intelligently.

2.5 Challenges in Software Development for Robotics

Despite the advancements in robotics software development, several challenges remain:

- **Real-Time Performance**: Many robotic applications require real-time performance, meaning that the system must respond to inputs without significant delays. Achieving real-time performance often requires careful optimization of code and system architecture.

- **Interoperability**: As robotics systems become more complex, ensuring that various software components work together seamlessly is crucial. Developers often face challenges in integrating software from different vendors or platforms.

- **Safety and Reliability**: Robotics applications, especially those in critical fields like healthcare and transportation, must meet stringent safety and reliability standards. Developing software that adheres to these standards while maintaining performance can be challenging.

2.6 Case Studies

To further illustrate the principles of software development in robotics, we can examine a few case studies:

- **Boston Dynamics' Atlas Robot**: The development of the Atlas robot showcases the integration of advanced software and hardware. The software controls its movements, enabling it to navigate complex environments, perform backflips, and even carry objects. The underlying software utilizes algorithms for balance, perception, and motion planning.

- **Tesla's Autopilot**: Tesla's Autopilot system exemplifies the use of sophisticated software to achieve autonomous driving. The system processes data from various sensors, including cameras and radar, to make real-time driving decisions. The continuous software updates improve performance and enhance safety features.

- **Da Vinci Surgical System**: The da Vinci Surgical System illustrates the critical role of software in healthcare robotics. Its software integrates precise control algorithms with real-time feedback from surgical instruments, allowing surgeons to perform minimally invasive procedures with exceptional accuracy.

Conclusion

In conclusion, software development is at the heart of robotic applications, enabling machines to perform a wide range of tasks autonomously and interactively. By utilizing various programming languages, methodologies, and frameworks, developers can create efficient and reliable robotic systems. While challenges remain, ongoing advancements in software engineering continue to drive innovation in the field of robotics, paving the way for future applications that were once considered science fiction.

3. Prototyping and Testing in Robotics Development

Prototyping and testing are integral stages in the development of robotic systems, serving as crucial processes that bridge the gap between design and production. These phases ensure that robotic systems function as intended, are safe to operate, and meet user requirements. This section will explore the significance of prototyping and testing in robotics, outlining different methodologies, tools, and examples that illustrate best practices in the field. By understanding these concepts, engineers and developers can improve the reliability and effectiveness of their robotic solutions.

3.1 The Importance of Prototyping in Robotics

Prototyping allows engineers to visualize their ideas and verify design concepts before committing to full-scale production. In robotics, prototypes can be categorized into several types, each serving different purposes:

- **Proof of Concept (PoC)**: A PoC prototype is built to demonstrate that a particular idea or concept is feasible. For instance, a team designing a robotic arm may create a simple model to show that their design can perform basic tasks like picking up objects.

- **Functional Prototype**: This type of prototype incorporates the core functionalities of the final product, allowing for more thorough testing and evaluation. An example could be a mobile robot designed to navigate through a maze, equipped with sensors and basic navigation algorithms.

- **Pre-production Prototype**: This prototype closely resembles the final product in terms of materials and design. It is often used for final testing and validation before mass production begins. For example, companies like Boston Dynamics create pre-production prototypes of their robots, such as Spot, to refine performance and durability.

3.2 Prototyping Methods

Several prototyping methods are employed in robotics, including:

- **Rapid Prototyping**: This method utilizes technologies such as 3D printing to create models quickly. Rapid prototyping enables engineers to iterate on designs efficiently, facilitating faster development cycles. For example, 3D-printed components for drones allow engineers to test new designs without the lengthy process of traditional manufacturing.

- **Simulation-Based Prototyping**: Simulation tools enable engineers to create virtual models of robotic systems, allowing for testing and analysis in a controlled environment. Software like Gazebo or V-REP helps visualize robotic interactions with the environment, enabling teams to refine algorithms before deploying them on physical robots.

- **Hardware-in-the-Loop (HIL) Prototyping**: HIL testing integrates real hardware components into the simulation environment. This allows engineers to evaluate how software interacts with physical systems in real-time, ensuring that designs perform correctly under various conditions. For instance, HIL testing is often used in autonomous vehicle development to assess control algorithms and sensor integration.

3.3 Testing Strategies in Robotics

Effective testing is critical to ensuring that robotic systems perform reliably in real-world environments. Common testing strategies include:

- **Unit Testing**: This involves testing individual components or modules of the robotic system in isolation. For example, testing the functionality of a robot's arm before integrating it with the control system ensures that each part works as intended.

- **Integration Testing**: After unit testing, integration testing examines how different components work together. This phase verifies that the interactions between hardware and software produce the desired outcomes. For instance, testing a robotic vacuum's navigation system with its obstacle detection sensors ensures that the robot can navigate around furniture effectively.

- **System Testing**: This comprehensive testing approach evaluates the entire robotic system's performance against specified requirements. System testing may involve assessing a robot's functionality in various environments and scenarios. For example, a warehouse robot may undergo system testing to determine how well it can navigate crowded aisles while picking items.

- **Field Testing**: This testing occurs in real-world conditions, allowing engineers to assess a robot's performance in actual operational environments. Field testing provides invaluable insights into how robots perform under various conditions. For instance, agricultural robots may be tested in fields to evaluate their ability to navigate uneven terrain and handle crops effectively.

3.4 Case Studies in Prototyping and Testing

To illustrate the importance of prototyping and testing in robotics, let's examine a few notable case studies:

- **NASA's Mars Rover**: The development of the Mars Rover involved extensive prototyping and testing to ensure that it could withstand the harsh conditions of space. Engineers created multiple prototypes and conducted rigorous testing, including simulations of Martian terrain, to ensure the rover could navigate safely and perform its scientific missions.

- **Boston Dynamics' Spot Robot**: The Spot robot underwent multiple prototyping phases, from early models to pre-production units. Extensive testing in various environments, including urban and industrial settings, allowed the team to refine Spot's mobility, stability, and ability to navigate complex obstacles effectively.

- **Robotic Surgery Systems**: Companies developing robotic surgery systems, such as the da Vinci Surgical System, engage in detailed prototyping and testing. These systems undergo rigorous evaluation in simulated surgical scenarios to ensure safety and precision before being approved for use in actual surgeries.

3.5 Tools and Technologies for Prototyping and Testing

Various tools and technologies are employed in the prototyping and testing phases of robotics development:

- **3D Printing**: As mentioned earlier, 3D printing technology facilitates rapid prototyping, enabling engineers to create complex parts and assemblies quickly. This technology is particularly beneficial in developing custom robotic components.

- **Simulation Software**: Tools like MATLAB, Simulink, and Gazebo are widely used for simulating robotic systems, allowing engineers to test algorithms and control strategies in a virtual environment before deployment.

- **Testing Frameworks**: Frameworks such as Robot Operating System (ROS) provide libraries and tools for developing and testing robotic applications. ROS allows for easy integration of various sensors and actuators, streamlining the testing process.

3.6 Challenges in Prototyping and Testing

Despite the advancements in prototyping and testing methodologies, several challenges persist:

- **Resource Limitations**: Prototyping can be resource-intensive, requiring significant time, expertise, and funding. Smaller robotics firms may struggle to access the necessary resources for thorough prototyping and testing.

- **Complexity of Integration**: As robotic systems become increasingly complex, integrating various components for testing can be challenging. Ensuring that all elements work together effectively requires careful planning and execution.

- **Safety Concerns**: Testing robots in real-world scenarios can pose safety risks, particularly when dealing with heavy machinery or autonomous vehicles. Developers must prioritize safety measures to protect both operators and the public during testing phases.

Conclusion

In conclusion, prototyping and testing are fundamental components of robotics development that ensure systems are efficient, safe, and reliable. By utilizing various methodologies and tools, engineers can validate their designs, improve performance, and address potential issues before full-scale production. Through continuous refinement and rigorous testing, the robotics industry can deliver innovative solutions that meet the evolving demands of various applications.

4. Design Considerations for Safety and Usability

In the rapidly evolving field of robotics, the design of robotic systems must prioritize both safety and usability. As robots increasingly integrate into various environments—ranging from manufacturing floors to homes—designers and engineers face the challenge of creating systems that not only perform tasks efficiently but also ensure the safety of users and the surrounding environment. This chapter delves into the critical considerations for designing robotic systems with an emphasis on safety protocols and user-friendly interfaces. By exploring best practices and real-world examples, we aim to provide insights into how to create robotic solutions that meet the highest standards of safety and usability.

4.1 Importance of Safety in Robotics Design

Safety is paramount in robotics, especially as robots are deployed in environments where they interact with humans and perform critical tasks. The importance of safety in robotic design can be illustrated through several key factors:

- **Risk Mitigation**: Identifying and mitigating potential hazards associated with robotic systems is crucial. For instance, industrial robots operating in factories must have safety measures in place to prevent accidents, such as collision detection systems that stop the robot when an object or person enters its path.

- **Regulatory Compliance**: Many regions have established safety standards and regulations that robotic systems must comply with, such as the ISO 10218 standard for industrial robots. These regulations help ensure that robots operate safely in diverse environments, providing a framework for designers to follow.

- **User Confidence**: A focus on safety fosters user confidence in robotic systems. When users trust that a robot is designed with their safety in mind, they are more likely to adopt the technology, leading to wider acceptance and integration of robotics in various sectors.

4.2 Safety Design Principles

Designing for safety involves implementing several principles that guide the development of robotic systems:

- **Fail-Safe Mechanisms**: Robots should be designed with fail-safe mechanisms that ensure they default to a safe state in the event of a malfunction. For example, an autonomous vehicle may be programmed to engage emergency brakes if a critical system failure occurs.

- **Redundant Systems**: Incorporating redundancy in critical components enhances safety. For instance, a robotic surgical system may have multiple sensors monitoring the position of surgical instruments, ensuring that if one sensor fails, others can take over to maintain accuracy.

- **Emergency Stop Controls**: All robotic systems should feature easily accessible emergency stop controls that allow operators to immediately halt operations in case of an emergency. This is especially important in industrial settings where robots work alongside human operators.

4.3 Usability in Robotics Design

Usability is equally important in robotics design, as it directly impacts user experience and the effectiveness of robotic systems. Key considerations for usability include:

- **User Interface Design**: The design of user interfaces (UIs) should prioritize simplicity and clarity. For example, a mobile robot used in healthcare may feature a touchscreen interface that allows staff to easily input commands and monitor the robot's status.

- **Intuitive Controls**: Robotic systems should have intuitive controls that align with user expectations. In collaborative robotics, where humans and robots work together, ensuring that the robot responds predictably to human commands is crucial for effective teamwork.

- **Training and Support**: Providing adequate training and support for users enhances usability. For instance, a manufacturer deploying robotic assembly lines should offer comprehensive training programs to ensure operators understand how to interact safely and efficiently with the robots.

4.4 Human-Robot Interaction (HRI)

The interaction between humans and robots (HRI) is a critical area of focus in usability design. Effective HRI can enhance both safety and usability through:

- **Clear Communication**: Robots should communicate their actions and intentions clearly to users. For example, a robotic vacuum cleaner may use visual or auditory signals to indicate when it is starting or stopping, allowing users to adjust their behavior accordingly.

- **Feedback Mechanisms**: Providing users with feedback about the robot's status enhances usability. For instance, a collaborative robot may have visual indicators (like LED lights) that signal when it is in operation or on standby, helping users understand its current state.

- **Adaptability**: Robots that can adapt to user preferences improve usability. For example, a personal assistant robot may learn a user's daily schedule and preferences, optimizing its interactions based on that information.

4.5 Case Studies in Safety and Usability Design

Examining case studies of successful robotic systems can provide valuable insights into effective design practices:

- **Kiva Systems (now Amazon Robotics)**: The Kiva mobile robots used in warehouses were designed with safety and usability in mind. They employ laser sensors to navigate safely around obstacles and human workers, demonstrating the importance of incorporating advanced safety features in logistics robots.

- **Robotic Surgical Systems**: The da Vinci Surgical System is a prime example of a robot designed for safety and usability in a critical environment. Its design includes redundant safety features and a user-friendly interface that allows surgeons to perform complex procedures with precision, enhancing both patient safety and surgical outcomes.

- **Assistive Robots for the Elderly**: Robots designed to assist elderly individuals, such as the Pepper robot, focus on usability by incorporating friendly designs and interactive interfaces. These robots are programmed to engage with users in a natural manner, improving user comfort and acceptance.

4.6 Tools and Techniques for Safety and Usability Testing

Testing is a crucial part of ensuring that robotic systems meet safety and usability standards. Several tools and techniques can aid in this process:

- **User-Centered Design (UCD)**: Employing UCD principles ensures that the design process is focused on the needs and experiences of users. Techniques such as usability testing and user feedback sessions can help refine robotic interfaces.

- **Safety Assessments**: Conducting thorough safety assessments, including hazard analysis and risk assessments, helps identify potential issues in robotic systems before deployment.

- **Simulation and Modeling**: Tools for simulation and modeling, such as MATLAB and Simulink, allow designers to evaluate safety and usability in a virtual environment before physical prototypes are built.

4.7 Challenges in Designing for Safety and Usability

Despite the emphasis on safety and usability, several challenges persist in the design process:

- **Balancing Complexity and Usability**: As robotic systems become more complex, ensuring that they remain user-friendly can be challenging. Designers must balance advanced functionality with ease of use to avoid overwhelming users.

- **Evolving Regulations**: Navigating the regulatory landscape for safety standards can be difficult, especially as new technologies emerge. Designers must stay informed about changing regulations to ensure compliance.

- **User Diversity**: Different users have varying levels of familiarity with technology, making it essential to design systems that accommodate a wide range of users, from experts to novices.

Conclusion

In summary, safety and usability are critical considerations in the design of robotic systems. By implementing safety design principles and focusing on user-friendly interfaces, engineers can create robotic solutions that not only perform efficiently but also ensure the well-being of users and their environments. Through case studies and best practices, this chapter underscores the importance of prioritizing safety and usability in robotics design, paving the way for successful integration and acceptance of robotic systems across various sectors.

5. Innovations in Materials and Manufacturing Techniques for Robots

The field of robotics is experiencing rapid advancements, particularly in materials and manufacturing techniques. Innovations in these areas are crucial for developing robots that are not only more efficient but also lighter, stronger, and more adaptable to various applications. As robots become integral to diverse industries, from healthcare to manufacturing, the need for advanced materials that enhance performance and durability is paramount. This chapter explores the latest innovations in materials and manufacturing techniques for robotics, emphasizing how these advancements impact robot design, functionality, and usability.

5.1 Advanced Materials in Robotics

The selection of materials in robotic design plays a significant role in determining the robot's performance, weight, and durability. Recent developments in material science have led to the emergence of several advanced materials that are transforming robotics.

- **Lightweight Composites**: Composite materials, such as carbon fiber and fiberglass, offer high strength-to-weight ratios, making them ideal for robotic structures. These materials are increasingly used in drones and robotic arms, allowing for increased mobility and reduced energy consumption. For example, the lightweight nature of carbon fiber helps drones achieve longer flight times while carrying heavier payloads.

- **Smart Materials**: Smart materials, which can change properties in response to external stimuli, are finding applications in robotics. Shape memory alloys (SMAs), for instance, can change shape when heated, allowing for the creation of soft robots that can adapt their form to different tasks. An example is the use of SMAs in robotic grippers that can securely hold various objects by adjusting their shape according to the object's contours.

- **Biomaterials**: In healthcare robotics, biomaterials that are biocompatible are crucial. These materials can interact safely with biological tissues, making them suitable for surgical robots. Innovations in biomaterials include hydrogels that mimic soft tissues, enabling robotic systems to perform delicate tasks in medical procedures.

5.2 Manufacturing Techniques

The manufacturing process of robots is undergoing significant transformations due to advancements in technology. These innovations are enabling more efficient production methods, reduced costs, and improved product quality.

- **Additive Manufacturing (3D Printing)**: Additive manufacturing has revolutionized how robotic components are produced. This technique allows for the creation of complex geometries that were previously difficult or impossible to achieve with traditional manufacturing methods. For example, 3D-printed robot parts can be customized for specific applications, such as creating lightweight exoskeletons for rehabilitation that are tailored to individual patients.

- **Automation in Manufacturing**: The use of robotics in manufacturing processes enhances productivity and precision. Robotic arms equipped with advanced sensors and AI algorithms can perform repetitive tasks with high accuracy, reducing human error. Companies like Tesla employ robots for assembly line processes, improving efficiency while maintaining high-quality standards.

- **Laser Cutting and Welding**: Innovations in laser cutting and welding technologies have streamlined the production of robotic components. Laser cutting allows for precise cuts in various materials, while advanced welding techniques ensure strong joints in robotic assemblies. These methods contribute to the overall structural integrity and performance of robotic systems.

5.3 Modular Robotics

Modular robotics is a design philosophy that emphasizes the use of interchangeable components or modules. This approach offers several advantages in terms of flexibility and scalability.

- **Reconfigurable Robots**: Modular robots can be easily reconfigured for different tasks, enhancing their versatility. For example, the M-Blocks developed by MIT are cube-shaped robots that can autonomously rearrange themselves to form different structures, demonstrating the potential of modular design in robotics.

- **Rapid Prototyping**: The use of modular components allows for rapid prototyping and testing of new designs. Engineers can quickly assemble and disassemble robots to experiment with different configurations, speeding up the development process.

- **Cost-Effective Solutions**: Modular robotics can reduce production costs as components can be mass-produced and easily replaced or upgraded. This approach is particularly beneficial in educational settings, where institutions can use modular kits for teaching robotics concepts.

5.4 Sustainability in Robotics

Sustainability is becoming an increasingly important consideration in the design and manufacturing of robots. Innovations in materials and processes are aimed at reducing environmental impact.

- **Recyclable Materials**: The use of recyclable materials in robotic construction contributes to sustainability. For instance, some companies are exploring the use of bioplastics derived from renewable resources to manufacture robot parts, reducing reliance on fossil fuels.

- **Energy-Efficient Manufacturing Processes**: Advances in manufacturing techniques, such as lean manufacturing, focus on minimizing waste and energy consumption during production. These practices not only lower costs but also reduce the carbon footprint of robotic systems.

- **Energy Harvesting Technologies**: Some robots are being designed to incorporate energy harvesting technologies, allowing them to generate power from their environment. For example, small robots can use piezoelectric materials to convert mechanical stress into electrical energy, extending their operational lifetime.

5.5 Case Studies

Examining case studies of companies and research institutions that are leading the way in materials and manufacturing innovations provides valuable insights:

- **Boston Dynamics**: Known for their advanced robotic systems, Boston Dynamics utilizes lightweight materials and cutting-edge manufacturing techniques to produce robots like Spot, a versatile quadruped designed for various applications, including inspections and data collection in hazardous environments.

- **DJI**: As a leader in drone technology, DJI employs advanced materials such as carbon fiber and innovative manufacturing processes to create lightweight and durable drones. Their products are known for their performance and reliability, showcasing the impact of material innovations in the robotics industry.

- **iRobot**: The company behind the Roomba vacuum cleaner focuses on integrating smart materials and manufacturing techniques to enhance the usability and efficiency of their robotic products. Their commitment to continuous innovation demonstrates how advancements in materials can lead to improved consumer robotics.

5.6 Challenges in Material and Manufacturing Innovations

Despite the advancements in materials and manufacturing techniques, several challenges remain:

- **Cost of Advanced Materials**: While advanced materials offer numerous benefits, they can be expensive to produce and integrate into robotic systems. This cost can be a barrier for smaller companies and startups looking to innovate in the robotics space.

- **Compatibility of Materials**: Ensuring compatibility between different materials used in robotic systems can be challenging. Designers must consider how materials interact with one another to avoid issues such as corrosion or structural weaknesses.

- **Sustainability Trade-offs**: While there is a push for sustainable materials and processes, achieving sustainability without compromising performance can be a delicate balance. Companies must invest in research to find solutions that meet both environmental and performance standards.

Conclusion

Innovations in materials and manufacturing techniques are shaping the future of robotics, enabling the development of more efficient, adaptable, and sustainable robotic systems. By leveraging advanced materials such as lightweight composites, smart materials, and biomaterials, alongside cutting-edge manufacturing processes like additive manufacturing and automation, engineers and designers can create robots that meet the demands of various industries. As the field continues to evolve, addressing challenges related to cost, compatibility, and sustainability will be essential for driving further advancements in robotics.

Chapter 5: Applications of Robotics

1. Overview of Robotics Applications in Various Industries
2. Robotics in Healthcare: Surgical Robots and Rehabilitation
3. Robotics in Manufacturing: Automation and Efficiency
4. The Role of Robotics in Logistics and Supply Chain
5. Future Applications and Market Trends

Chapter 5

Applications of Robotics

Introduction

The rapid advancement of robotics technology is transforming numerous industries, reshaping the way tasks are performed and services are delivered. As robots become more sophisticated and capable, their applications extend far beyond traditional manufacturing settings. This chapter explores the diverse applications of robotics across various sectors, highlighting the significant impact these technologies have on efficiency, safety, and productivity.

In healthcare, robotics is revolutionizing surgical procedures and rehabilitation therapies, improving patient outcomes and enhancing the precision of medical interventions. In manufacturing, robots are driving automation, optimizing production processes, and increasing operational efficiency, leading to significant cost savings and enhanced product quality. The logistics and supply chain industries are also leveraging robotics to streamline operations, reduce human error, and accelerate delivery times.

As we delve into the current applications of robotics, we will also examine emerging trends that signal the future direction of this dynamic field. From collaborative robots (cobots) working alongside human operators to advancements in artificial intelligence that enable autonomous decision-making, the potential for robotics to reshape various sectors is vast and continually evolving.

This chapter aims to provide a comprehensive overview of how robotics is currently being applied in key industries and the transformative effects these technologies are having on the economy and society as a whole. By understanding the landscape of robotics applications, we can better appreciate the opportunities and challenges that lie ahead in this rapidly evolving domain.

1. Overview of Robotics Applications in Various Industries

The integration of robotics across various industries has revolutionized the way businesses operate. As technology continues to advance, robots are becoming increasingly capable of performing complex tasks, thereby enhancing efficiency, productivity, and safety. This chapter provides a comprehensive overview of robotics applications in multiple sectors, including manufacturing, healthcare, agriculture, logistics, and more. By examining real-world examples, we will illustrate how robotics is transforming operations and driving innovation in these fields.

1.1 Robotics in Manufacturing

Manufacturing has traditionally been one of the primary domains for robotics applications. The use of robots in assembly lines, welding, painting, and material handling has significantly increased productivity and quality. For instance, automotive manufacturers like Toyota and Ford employ robotic arms for precise assembly tasks, allowing for faster production cycles and consistent quality control.

Example: Collaborative Robots (Cobots)

Collaborative robots, or cobots, are designed to work alongside human workers. These robots enhance efficiency by automating repetitive tasks while allowing humans to focus on more complex and creative aspects of production. A notable example is the Universal Robots UR series, which is widely used in small to medium-sized enterprises for tasks such as machine tending and packaging.

1.2 Robotics in Healthcare

The healthcare industry is witnessing a transformation driven by robotics, particularly in surgical procedures and patient care. Surgical robots, such as the da Vinci Surgical System, enable surgeons to perform minimally invasive procedures with enhanced precision and control.

Example: Robotic-Assisted Surgery

Robotic-assisted surgery allows for smaller incisions, reduced blood loss, and faster recovery times. The da Vinci system provides surgeons with 3D visualization and dexterity, improving outcomes for patients undergoing procedures such as prostatectomies and gynecologic surgeries.

1.3 Robotics in Agriculture

Robotics is increasingly making its mark in agriculture, helping to optimize processes and address labor shortages. Autonomous tractors, drones, and robotic harvesters are being employed to enhance productivity and efficiency on farms.

Example: Precision Agriculture

Robots equipped with advanced sensors can monitor crop health, assess soil conditions, and apply fertilizers or pesticides with pinpoint accuracy. For instance, the Harvest CROO Robotics strawberry-picking robot uses computer vision and machine learning to identify ripe strawberries and harvest them efficiently, reducing labor costs and increasing yield.

1.4 Robotics in Logistics and Supply Chain

The logistics and supply chain sectors are leveraging robotics to streamline operations, improve inventory management, and enhance delivery efficiency. Automated guided vehicles (AGVs) and drones are being deployed in warehouses and distribution centers.

Example: Amazon Robotics

Amazon uses robotics extensively in its fulfillment centers to optimize order processing and delivery. The Kiva robots move products to human workers, significantly reducing the time needed to locate items. This automation has enabled Amazon to meet the high demand for fast delivery while maintaining accuracy in order fulfillment.

1.5 Robotics in Service Industries

Beyond manufacturing and logistics, robotics is also making strides in service industries such as hospitality and customer service. Robots are being employed to assist in various tasks, from cleaning to customer interaction.

Example: Hospitality Robots

Hotels and restaurants are adopting robots to enhance customer experience and operational efficiency. For instance, the Henn-na Hotel in Japan employs robot staff for check-in, luggage handling, and even room service. These robots not only improve service speed but also attract guests interested in technological innovations.

1.6 Challenges and Considerations

While the benefits of robotics are significant, several challenges must be addressed. These include workforce displacement concerns, the high cost of implementation, and the need for skilled technicians to maintain and operate robotic systems. Moreover, the ethical implications of deploying robots in sensitive areas such as healthcare require careful consideration.

Conclusion

Robotics applications are diverse and continually evolving across various industries. From manufacturing and healthcare to agriculture and logistics, robots are driving innovation and improving efficiency. As technology progresses, the integration of robotics will likely expand further, offering new solutions to existing challenges and creating opportunities for growth in numerous sectors.

2. Robotics in Healthcare: Surgical Robots and Rehabilitation

The healthcare industry is undergoing a transformative shift, significantly driven by advancements in robotics technology. From enhancing surgical precision to improving rehabilitation outcomes, robotics is revolutionizing patient care and medical procedures. This chapter delves into the various applications of robotics in healthcare, focusing on surgical robots and rehabilitation technologies. We will explore the benefits and challenges associated with these innovations, supported by real-world examples that highlight their impact on patient outcomes and the healthcare ecosystem.

2.1 The Rise of Surgical Robots

Surgical robots have emerged as a game-changing technology in the operating room, enabling minimally invasive procedures with unparalleled precision. These robotic systems are designed to assist surgeons in performing complex operations with greater accuracy, flexibility, and control.

Example: The da Vinci Surgical System

One of the most well-known surgical robots is the da Vinci Surgical System, developed by Intuitive Surgical. This system features a robotic console that allows surgeons to manipulate instruments through small incisions using 3D visualization and high-definition imaging. The da Vinci system is widely used in urology, gynecology, and thoracic surgeries. Studies have shown that surgeries performed with this robot result in less postoperative pain, shorter hospital stays, and quicker recovery times for patients.

2.2 Benefits of Surgical Robots

The integration of surgical robots into operating rooms offers several key benefits:

- **Minimally Invasive Procedures:** Robotic-assisted surgeries often require smaller incisions, leading to reduced blood loss and lower infection rates.

- **Enhanced Precision:** Surgical robots allow for more precise movements than human hands, especially in delicate procedures.

- **Improved Visualization:** The use of advanced imaging technology provides surgeons with a clearer view of the surgical site, aiding in decision-making during complex procedures.

- **Reduced Recovery Time:** Patients typically experience faster recovery and less postoperative discomfort, allowing for earlier return to normal activities.

2.3 Challenges and Considerations

Despite their advantages, the adoption of surgical robots presents challenges. High costs associated with robotic systems can limit access, particularly in smaller healthcare facilities. Additionally, the learning curve for surgeons can be steep, necessitating specialized training to achieve proficiency in robotic-assisted techniques. There are also concerns regarding the reliability and maintenance of these complex systems.

2.4 Robotics in Rehabilitation

Beyond surgical applications, robotics is also making significant strides in rehabilitation. Robotic rehabilitation systems are designed to assist patients in recovering from injuries, surgeries, or neurological conditions.

Example: Robotic Exoskeletons

Robotic exoskeletons are wearable devices that aid individuals with mobility impairments in regaining movement. One prominent example is the EksoGT exoskeleton, which allows patients with lower limb disabilities to stand and walk. This device is particularly beneficial for individuals recovering from spinal cord injuries or strokes.

2.5 Benefits of Robotic Rehabilitation

The use of robotic systems in rehabilitation offers numerous advantages:

- **Personalized Therapy:** Robotic rehabilitation can be tailored to individual patient needs, allowing for customized exercise programs that adapt to progress.

- **Increased Engagement:** The interactive nature of robotic rehabilitation often motivates patients to participate actively in their recovery process.

- **Consistent Support:** Robots provide consistent assistance, enabling patients to practice movements repetitively, which is crucial for neural recovery and muscle strength.

- **Real-time Feedback:** Many robotic rehabilitation systems offer real-time feedback to patients and therapists, helping to track progress and adjust therapy plans as needed.

2.6 Challenges in Robotic Rehabilitation

While robotic rehabilitation presents promising opportunities, several challenges exist:

- **High Costs:** Like surgical robots, rehabilitation robots can be expensive, limiting access for some patients.

- **Integration into Existing Therapy Programs:** Successfully incorporating robotic rehabilitation into traditional therapy can be challenging and requires collaboration among healthcare providers.

- **Patient Acceptance:** Some patients may be hesitant to engage with robotic systems, fearing a lack of human interaction during their recovery process.

2.7 Future Directions in Healthcare Robotics

The future of robotics in healthcare is bright, with ongoing research and development aimed at improving existing technologies and creating new solutions. Emerging trends include:

- **Telepresence Surgery:** Advances in teleoperated robotic systems may allow surgeons to perform operations remotely, expanding access to expert care in underserved areas.

- **AI and Machine Learning:** The integration of artificial intelligence and machine learning can enhance robotic systems, enabling them to adapt to individual patient needs and improve outcomes.

- **Wearable Robotics:** Innovations in wearable technology will likely lead to more sophisticated exoskeletons and rehabilitation devices that are more user-friendly and effective.

Conclusion

Robotics is playing an increasingly vital role in the healthcare sector, particularly in surgical applications and rehabilitation. As these technologies continue to evolve, they promise to enhance patient care, improve surgical outcomes, and support individuals in their recovery journeys. However, addressing the challenges associated with implementation and access will be crucial for maximizing the benefits of robotics in healthcare.

3. Robotics in Manufacturing: Automation and Efficiency

The manufacturing sector has undergone a remarkable transformation over the past few decades, largely due to the integration of robotics and automation technologies. Robotics in manufacturing refers to the use of robotic systems to perform tasks traditionally done by human labor, enhancing productivity, efficiency, and accuracy. This chapter explores the various applications of robotics in manufacturing, highlighting their role in automation, improving efficiency, and driving industry innovations. Through real-world examples, we will illustrate how robotic systems have revolutionized manufacturing processes across different industries and discuss the benefits and challenges associated with their implementation.

3.1 The Evolution of Robotics in Manufacturing

The journey of robotics in manufacturing began in the mid-20th century when the first industrial robots were introduced. These early robots were primarily used for repetitive tasks such as welding and assembly. Over time, advancements in technology have expanded their capabilities and applications, allowing them to perform more complex tasks with precision and reliability.

Example: The Unimate Robot

One of the first industrial robots was the Unimate, developed by George Devol and later commercialized by General Motors in the 1960s. This robot was used for die-casting operations and revolutionized the manufacturing process by improving efficiency and safety. The success of Unimate paved the way for the widespread adoption of robotics in manufacturing, leading to the development of more advanced robotic systems.

3.2 Benefits of Robotics in Manufacturing

Robotics has brought numerous advantages to the manufacturing sector, including:

- **Increased Productivity:** Robots can operate continuously without fatigue, leading to higher production rates and reduced cycle times. For example, automotive assembly lines use robots to perform repetitive tasks like welding, painting, and assembly, significantly increasing throughput.

- **Improved Precision and Quality:** Robotic systems are capable of performing tasks with high precision, reducing the likelihood of errors and ensuring consistent quality. For instance, in electronics manufacturing, robots are used for delicate assembly processes, such as placing tiny components on circuit boards.

- **Enhanced Safety:** By automating dangerous tasks, such as heavy lifting or working in hazardous environments, robots help reduce workplace injuries. For example, robots are employed in the construction industry for tasks like bricklaying and concrete pouring, minimizing the risk to human workers.

- **Cost Savings:** While the initial investment in robotic systems can be significant, the long-term cost savings through increased efficiency, reduced labor costs, and minimized waste can be substantial. Manufacturers can achieve a quick return on investment (ROI) by implementing robotics in their operations.

3.3 Types of Robotic Applications in Manufacturing

Robotics in manufacturing can be categorized into various applications, each tailored to specific tasks:

- **Assembly Robots:** Used for assembling components into final products, these robots can perform tasks such as screwing, fitting, and welding. The KUKA Robotics company, for instance, provides versatile assembly robots for automotive manufacturing.

- **Material Handling Robots:** These robots are designed for transporting materials within a facility, reducing the need for manual labor. Automated guided vehicles (AGVs) are commonly used in warehouses and factories for moving goods.

- **Inspection and Quality Control Robots:** Equipped with vision systems, these robots can inspect products for defects and ensure quality standards are met. For example, companies like Cognex provide vision systems integrated with robots for real-time quality control.

- **Collaborative Robots (Cobots):** Unlike traditional industrial robots, cobots are designed to work alongside human operators safely. They are used in various tasks, from assembly to packaging, enhancing human-robot collaboration in manufacturing settings.

3.4 Real-World Examples of Robotics in Manufacturing

- **Automotive Manufacturing:** Companies like Tesla utilize advanced robotics in their production lines to automate tasks such as welding, painting, and assembly. This not only speeds up the production process but also ensures high-quality standards.

- **Electronics Manufacturing:** Foxconn, a major electronics manufacturer, employs thousands of robots to assemble smartphones and other electronic devices. The use of robotics has improved efficiency and reduced assembly time.

- **Food and Beverage Industry:** Robotics is increasingly used in food processing and packaging. For example, the Boston Dynamics Stretch robot is designed for warehouse automation in the food and beverage sector, enabling efficient palletizing and packaging.

3.5 Challenges in Implementing Robotics in Manufacturing

Despite the numerous benefits, the integration of robotics in manufacturing poses several challenges:

- **High Initial Costs:** The upfront investment in robotic systems can be substantial, making it difficult for small and medium-sized enterprises (SMEs) to adopt this technology.

- **Skills Gap:** The rapid advancement of robotics requires a skilled workforce capable of operating and maintaining these systems. Companies may face challenges in finding and training employees with the necessary technical skills.

- **Integration with Existing Systems:** Successfully integrating robotic systems into existing manufacturing processes can be complex and may require significant changes to workflows.

- **Job Displacement Concerns:** The increased use of robots in manufacturing raises concerns about job displacement for human workers. Companies must address these concerns and consider retraining programs to upskill their workforce.

3.6 Future Trends in Robotics in Manufacturing

The future of robotics in manufacturing is promising, with several trends emerging:

- **AI and Machine Learning Integration:** The incorporation of artificial intelligence (AI) and machine learning will enable robots to learn from data and adapt to changing environments, improving their efficiency and flexibility.

- **Enhanced Connectivity:** The rise of the Internet of Things (IoT) will allow robots to communicate with other machines and systems, leading to smarter manufacturing processes and predictive maintenance.

- **Customization and Flexibility:** Manufacturers are increasingly seeking flexible robotic solutions that can adapt to changing product designs and production schedules. Collaborative robots will play a vital role in enabling this flexibility.

- **Sustainability Efforts:** Robotics can contribute to sustainable manufacturing practices by optimizing resource usage, reducing waste, and improving energy efficiency in production processes.

Conclusion

Robotics has become an integral part of modern manufacturing, driving automation and efficiency across various industries. By enhancing productivity, improving quality, and ensuring workplace safety, robotic systems are reshaping the manufacturing landscape. However, addressing the challenges associated with implementation and workforce adaptation will be crucial for maximizing the benefits of robotics in manufacturing. As technology continues to advance, the potential for robotics to transform the manufacturing sector will only grow.

4. The Role of Robotics in Logistics and Supply Chain

In the modern era of globalization and e-commerce, the logistics and supply chain sectors have become increasingly complex and dynamic. The growing demand for faster, more efficient delivery of goods has necessitated the adoption of innovative technologies, among which robotics plays a pivotal role. Robotics in logistics encompasses the use of automated systems and machines to enhance the efficiency and effectiveness of supply chain operations, from warehousing to transportation. This chapter delves into the significant contributions of robotics in logistics and supply chain management, exploring various applications, benefits, challenges, and future trends. Through real-world examples, we will illustrate how robotic systems have transformed logistics operations, driving improvements in productivity and service delivery.

4.1 Evolution of Robotics in Logistics

The application of robotics in logistics has evolved significantly over the years. Initially, logistics operations relied heavily on manual labor, which was often time-consuming and prone to errors. The introduction of robotics began in the late 20th century, primarily focused on automating specific tasks within warehouses and distribution centers.

Example: Automated Guided Vehicles (AGVs)

One of the earliest forms of robotics in logistics was the implementation of Automated Guided Vehicles (AGVs). These vehicles, which navigate predetermined paths to transport goods within warehouses, began to gain popularity in the 1960s. AGVs improved operational efficiency by reducing manual handling and transportation time, marking the beginning of a new era in logistics automation.

4.2 Benefits of Robotics in Logistics and Supply Chain

The integration of robotics into logistics and supply chain management offers numerous advantages, including:

- **Increased Efficiency:** Robotics significantly speeds up logistics operations. Automated systems can operate around the clock without fatigue, leading to higher throughput. For instance, Amazon utilizes robotic systems in its fulfillment centers to optimize order picking and packing, resulting in faster delivery times.

- **Cost Reduction:** While the initial investment in robotic technology can be substantial, long-term savings can be achieved through reduced labor costs, minimized errors, and optimized resource utilization. According to a study by McKinsey, companies that adopt robotics can lower logistics costs by up to 20%.

- **Enhanced Accuracy:** Robotic systems are programmed to perform tasks with high precision, reducing the likelihood of errors in inventory management and order fulfillment. This accuracy is critical in preventing stockouts and ensuring customer satisfaction.

- **Improved Safety:** By automating dangerous tasks, such as heavy lifting and transporting hazardous materials, robots help minimize workplace injuries. For example, warehouse robots designed for transporting heavy goods reduce the risk of injuries associated with manual lifting.

- **Scalability:** Robotics allows logistics companies to easily scale their operations in response to fluctuating demand. Automated systems can be deployed quickly and efficiently, enabling companies to adapt to changing market conditions.

4.3 Applications of Robotics in Logistics and Supply Chain

Robotics has found applications across various facets of logistics and supply chain management:

- **Warehouse Automation:** Robotic systems are extensively used for tasks such as sorting, picking, packing, and inventory management. For example, Ocado, an online grocery retailer, employs a sophisticated robotic system that automates the entire warehouse process, from receiving orders to picking and dispatching.

- **Transportation and Delivery:** Robotics is transforming last-mile delivery through the use of autonomous vehicles and drones. Companies like Waymo and Amazon Prime Air are exploring the use of autonomous delivery vehicles and drones to expedite the delivery process and reduce costs.

- **Inventory Management:** Robotic systems equipped with advanced sensing and imaging technologies can monitor inventory levels in real-time. For instance, Walmart employs shelf-scanning robots to ensure accurate inventory counts and detect out-of-stock items, improving replenishment processes.

- **Sorting and Packaging:** Automated sorting systems streamline the packaging process by accurately sorting products based on destination. Companies like FedEx and UPS utilize robotic systems to enhance their sorting operations, ensuring timely deliveries.

4.4 Real-World Examples of Robotics in Logistics

- **Amazon Fulfillment Centers:** Amazon has set the benchmark for robotics in logistics with its use of Kiva robots to transport products throughout its massive fulfillment centers. These robots work alongside human workers, enhancing efficiency and reducing order processing time.

- **Zebra Technologies:** Zebra Technologies offers mobile robotics solutions for warehouse operations, enabling real-time inventory management and tracking. Their robotic systems help optimize inventory accuracy and streamline order fulfillment processes.

- **DHL Robotics:** DHL has integrated robotics into its logistics operations, employing robotic systems for picking and packing in its warehouses. Their use of robots has significantly improved operational efficiency and reduced order processing times.

4.5 Challenges in Implementing Robotics in Logistics

Despite the benefits, implementing robotics in logistics presents several challenges:

- **High Initial Investment:** The cost of acquiring and integrating robotic systems can be a significant barrier for many logistics companies, particularly small and medium-sized enterprises (SMEs).

- **Integration with Legacy Systems:** Many logistics companies operate on legacy systems, making it challenging to integrate new robotic technologies seamlessly. This integration requires careful planning and investment in technology.

- **Workforce Training:** The transition to automated systems necessitates retraining the workforce to work alongside robots. Companies must invest in training programs to ensure that employees have the necessary skills to operate and maintain robotic systems.

- **Maintenance and Downtime:** Robotic systems require regular maintenance to ensure optimal performance. Unplanned downtime can disrupt logistics operations and impact service delivery.

4.6 Future Trends in Robotics in Logistics

The future of robotics in logistics and supply chain management is bright, with several trends emerging:

- **Increased Use of Artificial Intelligence:** AI technologies will enhance the capabilities of robotic systems, enabling them to learn from data, adapt to changing conditions, and optimize operations further.

- **Collaborative Robots (Cobots):** The use of cobots, designed to work alongside human operators, will become more prevalent in logistics operations, improving efficiency and safety.

- **Expansion of Autonomous Delivery Solutions:** The development of autonomous delivery vehicles and drones will revolutionize last-mile delivery, providing faster and more cost-effective solutions for logistics companies.

- **Sustainability Initiatives:** Robotics can contribute to sustainable logistics practices by optimizing transportation routes, reducing energy consumption, and minimizing waste in supply chain operations.

Conclusion

Robotics plays a vital role in modern logistics and supply chain management, driving efficiency, accuracy, and safety across various operations. From warehouse automation to last-mile delivery, robotic systems are transforming how goods are managed and delivered. However, addressing the challenges associated with implementation and workforce adaptation will be essential for maximizing the benefits of robotics in logistics. As technology continues to evolve, the potential for robotics to reshape the logistics landscape will only increase, paving the way for more efficient and sustainable supply chain practices.

5. Future Applications and Market Trends

As robotics technology continues to evolve rapidly, its applications across various industries are expanding dramatically. The logistics sector, in particular, stands at the forefront of this evolution, leveraging advancements in automation, artificial intelligence, and machine learning to enhance operational efficiency and service delivery. This chapter delves into the future applications of robotics in logistics and supply chain management, examining the emerging trends that are expected to shape the industry in the coming years. By exploring real-world examples and analyzing market dynamics, we aim to provide insights into how robotics will redefine logistics operations and influence market trajectories.

5.1 Emerging Technologies in Robotics

The future of robotics in logistics is largely driven by the emergence of innovative technologies that enhance the capabilities and functionalities of robotic systems. Key advancements include:

- **Artificial Intelligence (AI) and Machine Learning:** The integration of AI and machine learning algorithms allows robots to learn from data, adapt to changing environments, and improve decision-making processes. These technologies enhance the operational efficiency of robotic systems by enabling them to optimize tasks such as routing, inventory management, and predictive maintenance.

Example: Predictive Analytics in Robotics

Companies like IBM are leveraging AI and machine learning to create predictive analytics tools that help logistics companies anticipate demand fluctuations and optimize inventory levels. By analyzing historical data and market trends, these tools enable more informed decision-making.

- **Advanced Sensing Technologies:** Robotics is increasingly utilizing sophisticated sensors and imaging technologies, such as LiDAR, computer vision, and ultrasonic sensors. These advancements enable robots to perceive their environment more accurately and interact effectively with dynamic surroundings.

Example: Autonomous Forklifts

Autonomous forklifts equipped with advanced sensors can navigate warehouse environments, avoid obstacles, and transport goods without human intervention. Companies like Toyota Material Handling have developed such systems to improve operational efficiency in logistics facilities.

- **Collaborative Robotics (Cobots):** Cobots are designed to work alongside human operators, enhancing productivity and safety in logistics operations. Unlike traditional industrial robots, which operate in isolation, cobots can collaborate with workers on various tasks, such as order picking and packing.

Example: Fetch Robotics

Fetch Robotics offers a range of collaborative robots that assist warehouse workers in material handling tasks. By reducing the physical strain on workers, cobots help improve workplace safety while increasing operational throughput.

5.2 Robotics in Last-Mile Delivery

One of the most significant trends in logistics is the increasing use of robotics for last-mile delivery. The demand for faster and more efficient delivery services, fueled by e-commerce growth, is driving innovation in this area. Key developments include:

- **Autonomous Delivery Vehicles:** Companies are investing in autonomous vehicles that can transport goods directly to customers' doorsteps. These vehicles are equipped with advanced navigation systems and sensors, allowing them to navigate urban environments safely.

Example: Waymo

Waymo, a subsidiary of Alphabet Inc., is testing autonomous delivery vehicles in various cities. By leveraging AI and machine learning, Waymo's vehicles can adapt to real-time traffic conditions and optimize delivery routes, enhancing the efficiency of last-mile logistics.

- **Drones for Delivery:** The use of drones for package delivery is gaining traction, especially in urban areas where traditional delivery methods may face congestion. Drones offer a fast and cost-effective solution for transporting goods over short distances.

Example: Amazon Prime Air

Amazon is actively developing its Prime Air drone delivery service, aiming to deliver packages to customers within 30 minutes. The company is investing heavily in drone technology to enhance its logistics capabilities and improve customer satisfaction.

- **Robotic Delivery Bots:** Small, ground-based robotic delivery units are becoming increasingly popular for delivering goods in urban environments. These robots can navigate sidewalks and streets, delivering packages directly to consumers.

Example: Starship Technologies

Starship Technologies operates a fleet of delivery robots that transport food and groceries in cities. These robots are designed to navigate autonomously, providing a convenient delivery solution for local businesses and customers.

5.3 Sustainability and Robotics

As environmental concerns continue to grow, sustainability is becoming a significant focus in the logistics industry. Robotics technology can contribute to more sustainable practices in several ways:

- **Energy Efficiency:** Automated systems can optimize energy consumption in logistics operations. For example, robotic systems can be programmed to operate during off-peak hours when energy costs are lower.

Example: Green Logistics with Robotics

Companies like DHL are implementing robotics in their warehouses to minimize energy usage. By automating repetitive tasks, DHL has been able to reduce its carbon footprint while maintaining high service levels.

- **Reduction of Waste:** Robotics can help minimize waste in supply chain processes by optimizing inventory management and reducing overproduction. By accurately forecasting demand and managing stock levels, companies can avoid excess inventory.

Example: Lean Robotics

Lean Robotics focuses on streamlining logistics operations to minimize waste. By integrating robotic systems into their processes, companies can achieve leaner supply chains, ultimately leading to lower waste levels.

- **Sustainable Packaging Solutions:** Robotics can also contribute to sustainable packaging practices by automating the packaging process to reduce material usage and promote eco-friendly materials.

Example: Eco-Friendly Packaging Robots

Companies like Packsize use robotic systems to create custom packaging solutions that minimize waste and improve sustainability. By automating the packaging process, they help companies reduce their environmental impact.

5.4 Market Trends and Predictions

The logistics robotics market is poised for significant growth in the coming years. According to recent market research, the global logistics automation market is expected to reach USD 60 billion by 2027, growing at a CAGR of 12.4% during the forecast period. Key trends driving this growth include:

- **Increased Investment in Robotics:** Companies are increasingly investing in robotic systems to enhance operational efficiency and remain competitive in the market. This trend is expected to accelerate as more businesses recognize the long-term benefits of automation.

- **Expansion of E-Commerce:** The continued growth of e-commerce is fueling demand for advanced logistics solutions. Robotics will play a crucial role in helping logistics companies meet the rising expectations for fast and efficient delivery.

- **Integration of Advanced Technologies:** The convergence of robotics with other advanced technologies, such as IoT and big data analytics, will further enhance the capabilities of logistics operations. This integration will enable real-time tracking, predictive analytics, and improved decision-making.

- **Adoption of Robotic Process Automation (RPA):** RPA is gaining traction in logistics operations, automating repetitive tasks and improving operational efficiency. This trend will continue to expand as logistics companies seek to streamline their processes and reduce operational costs.

Conclusion

The future of robotics in logistics and supply chain management is promising, driven by advancements in technology and the increasing demand for efficiency and sustainability. From autonomous delivery vehicles to collaborative robots, the applications of robotics are transforming logistics operations and reshaping the market landscape. As companies continue to invest in robotics and embrace innovation, the logistics industry will become more agile, efficient, and responsive to changing customer needs.

Chapter 6: Leading Companies in the Robotics Industry

1. Overview of Major Robotics Manufacturers
2. Case Studies of Innovative Robotics Companies
3. Competitive Landscape and Market Share
4. Strategic Partnerships and Collaborations in Robotics
5. Future Competitors and Emerging Startups

Chapter 6

Leading Companies in the Robotics Industry

Introduction

The robotics industry has experienced remarkable growth and transformation over the past few decades, driven by advancements in technology, increasing automation demands, and the need for efficient solutions across various sectors. This chapter provides an in-depth exploration of the leading companies that have significantly shaped the robotics landscape. By examining major robotics manufacturers, innovative case studies, and the competitive dynamics within the market, we aim to highlight the pivotal role these organizations play in driving innovation and progress in the industry.

The chapter begins with an overview of the major robotics manufacturers, focusing on their contributions, technological advancements, and market positions. This section sets the foundation for understanding the diverse landscape of robotics and the key players that dominate it.

Following the overview, we delve into case studies of innovative robotics companies that have successfully pushed the boundaries of what is possible in the field. These case studies illustrate how creativity, research, and development have led to groundbreaking technologies and applications, providing insights into the factors that contribute to their success.

The competitive landscape is another crucial aspect of this chapter. We will analyze market share distribution among leading companies, highlighting trends and shifts that characterize the industry. Understanding the competitive dynamics will shed light on the strategic maneuvers these companies employ to maintain their positions and drive growth.

Additionally, we explore the significance of strategic partnerships and collaborations in the robotics sector. As technology continues to evolve, companies increasingly recognize the value of working together to leverage complementary strengths and resources. This section will showcase examples of successful collaborations and their impact on innovation and market expansion.

Finally, we look ahead to the future of the robotics industry, identifying emerging startups and potential competitors that are poised to disrupt the market. By recognizing these new entrants and their innovative approaches, we can better understand the evolving landscape and the opportunities that lie ahead for established players and newcomers alike.

In summary, this chapter provides a comprehensive overview of the leading companies in the robotics industry, examining their contributions, competitive strategies, and the collaborative efforts that shape the future of robotics. Through this exploration, we aim to highlight the dynamic nature of the robotics landscape and the essential role these companies play in driving technological advancements and industry growth.

1. Overview of Major Robotics Manufacturers

The robotics industry is marked by a diverse array of manufacturers that have emerged as leaders in the development and application of robotic technologies. These companies range from long-established giants in automation to innovative startups pushing the boundaries of robotics across various sectors. In this section, we will explore the major robotics manufacturers, their core competencies, the technologies they develop, and their contributions to the industry. By examining key players in the market, we aim to provide a comprehensive overview of how these companies are shaping the future of robotics.

1.1 Key Robotics Manufacturers

1.1.1 ABB

ABB is a pioneering force in the robotics industry, known for its advanced industrial automation solutions. Founded in 1988, ABB has established itself as a leader in manufacturing and developing industrial robots used in automotive, electronics, and consumer goods industries. The company's robotic arms are designed for precision, speed, and reliability, making them indispensable in assembly lines and manufacturing processes.

Example: The ABB IRB 6700 is a versatile industrial robot that provides high performance in various applications, from welding to packaging. Its high payload capacity and reach make it suitable for heavy-duty tasks, helping companies improve efficiency and reduce production costs.

1.1.2 Fanuc

Fanuc, established in 1956 in Japan, is a major player in the robotics sector, specializing in CNC (Computer Numerical Control) systems and industrial robots. The company has a vast portfolio of robots, including articulated arms and collaborative robots (cobots) designed to work alongside humans.

Example: The Fanuc CR-35iA is a collaborative robot with a payload capacity of 35 kg, allowing it to perform tasks that require strength while ensuring safety in human-robot collaboration scenarios. This model has been widely adopted in various industries, including electronics and automotive manufacturing.

1.1.3 KUKA

KUKA, a German manufacturer founded in 1898, is known for its innovative robotic solutions and automation technology. The company produces a wide range of industrial robots, including those used in automotive assembly, electronics manufacturing, and healthcare.

Example: The KUKA LBR iiwa is a lightweight collaborative robot designed for delicate tasks. Its advanced sensors and flexible programming make it suitable for applications requiring high precision, such as assembly and quality inspection.

1.1.4 Yaskawa

Yaskawa Electric Corporation, established in 1915, is a global leader in industrial automation and robotics. The company's Motoman series of robots is renowned for its versatility and adaptability across various manufacturing sectors.

Example: The Yaskawa Motoman MH50 is an industrial robot designed for heavy payloads, making it ideal for tasks like welding, material handling, and assembly. Its high-speed capabilities contribute to increased productivity on assembly lines.

1.1.5 Universal Robots

Universal Robots, founded in 2005 in Denmark, specializes in collaborative robots that can safely work alongside humans. The company has revolutionized the robotics industry by making automation accessible to small and medium-sized enterprises.

Example: The UR5e is a lightweight collaborative robot designed for flexibility and ease of use. It can be programmed for various applications, from assembly to packaging, making it a popular choice for businesses seeking to enhance efficiency without significant investment.

1.2 Emerging Players in Robotics

1.2.1 Boston Dynamics

Founded in 1992 as a spin-off from MIT, Boston Dynamics is renowned for its cutting-edge robotics technologies, focusing on mobility and versatility. The company gained fame for its robotic prototypes like Spot, a quadrupedal robot capable of navigating complex terrains.

Example: Spot has been used in various applications, including construction site inspections and remote monitoring, showcasing the potential of agile robots in real-world scenarios.

1.2.2 Clearpath Robotics

Clearpath Robotics, a Canadian company founded in 2009, specializes in autonomous mobile robots for research and industrial applications. The company's robots are designed to navigate challenging environments, making them valuable in logistics and warehousing.

Example: The Clearpath Otto is an autonomous mobile robot designed for material handling in warehouses. Its ability to navigate without human intervention increases efficiency in supply chain operations.

1.3 Factors Influencing Manufacturer Success

1.3.1 Technological Innovation

Continuous technological innovation is a critical factor for success in the robotics industry. Leading manufacturers invest heavily in research and development to create cutting-edge solutions that meet the evolving needs of their customers.

1.3.2 Market Demand

The demand for automation solutions in various sectors, including manufacturing, healthcare, and logistics, drives the growth of robotics manufacturers. Companies that can quickly adapt to market trends and customer requirements are more likely to thrive.

1.3.3 Strategic Partnerships

Collaborations with other technology firms, research institutions, and industry players enhance manufacturers' capabilities and market reach. Strategic partnerships allow companies to leverage complementary strengths and drive innovation.

Conclusion

The robotics industry is characterized by a diverse array of manufacturers, each contributing uniquely to the evolution of robotic technologies. Companies like ABB, Fanuc, KUKA, Yaskawa, and Universal Robots lead the charge in industrial robotics, while emerging players like Boston Dynamics and Clearpath Robotics push the boundaries of innovation. As the demand for automation continues to grow across various sectors, understanding the dynamics of these major manufacturers will be essential for grasping the future of robotics.

2. Case Studies of Innovative Robotics Companies

Introduction

In the rapidly evolving field of robotics, several companies have distinguished themselves through innovation, pioneering technologies, and successful implementations across various industries. This section presents detailed case studies of innovative robotics companies, focusing on their unique approaches, key projects, and the impact of their solutions on their respective industries. By analyzing these case studies, we can gain insights into the factors that contribute to success in the robotics sector and the emerging trends shaping the future of this dynamic field.

2.1 Case Study: Boston Dynamics

2.1.1 Overview

Boston Dynamics, founded in 1992, is a robotics company that has gained global recognition for its advanced mobile robots. Known for their remarkable agility and versatility, Boston Dynamics' robots are designed to perform tasks in complex and unpredictable environments.

2.1.2 Key Innovations

Boston Dynamics has developed several iconic robots, including:

- **Spot:** A quadrupedal robot capable of navigating various terrains and performing tasks such as inspection, surveying, and data collection. Spot is equipped with advanced sensors and cameras, enabling it to operate autonomously or be remotely controlled.

- **Atlas:** A bipedal humanoid robot designed for tasks requiring human-like mobility and dexterity. Atlas can navigate rough terrain, climb stairs, and perform complex movements, showcasing the potential of humanoid robots in various applications.

2.1.3 Impact on Industries

Boston Dynamics' robots have found applications in industries such as construction, logistics, and military. For instance, Spot has been used in construction site inspections to improve safety and efficiency by reducing the need for human workers in hazardous environments. Similarly, Atlas has been employed in research and development projects to explore the capabilities of humanoid robots.

2.2 Case Study: Universal Robots

2.2.1 Overview

Universal Robots, founded in 2005 in Denmark, specializes in collaborative robots (cobots) designed to work alongside human operators. The company aims to make automation accessible to small and medium-sized enterprises (SMEs) by offering user-friendly and versatile robotic solutions.

2.2.2 Key Innovations

Universal Robots' product lineup includes several models, such as:

- **UR3e:** A compact and lightweight collaborative robot suitable for tasks like assembly, quality inspection, and packaging. The UR3e can be easily programmed by operators without extensive technical expertise, making it ideal for SMEs.

- **UR10e:** A larger cobot designed for heavier payloads, allowing it to handle tasks such as palletizing and machine tending.

2.2.3 Impact on Industries

Universal Robots has transformed automation in SMEs by providing cost-effective solutions that enhance productivity. Many businesses have adopted cobots to automate repetitive tasks, freeing up human workers to focus on more complex activities. For example, a small electronics manufacturer successfully integrated UR cobots into its production line, resulting in a significant increase in output while maintaining product quality.

2.3 Case Study: KUKA

2.3.1 Overview

KUKA, a German robotics manufacturer established in 1898, is renowned for its innovative automation solutions. The company has a strong presence in industries such as automotive, electronics, and healthcare.

2.3.2 Key Innovations

KUKA has developed a range of robots, including:

- **KUKA LBR iiwa:** A lightweight collaborative robot designed for sensitive applications. The LBR iiwa is equipped with force sensors that allow it to work safely alongside humans, making it suitable for assembly and quality control tasks.

- **KUKA KMR iiwa:** An autonomous mobile robot that combines the LBR iiwa with a mobile platform. This robot can navigate complex environments, providing flexibility in industrial settings.

2.3.3 Impact on Industries

KUKA's robots have played a significant role in automating production processes in the automotive industry. For instance, KUKA robots are widely used in assembly lines to perform tasks like welding, painting, and material handling, resulting in increased efficiency and reduced production costs.

2.4 Case Study: Clearpath Robotics

2.4.1 Overview

Clearpath Robotics, founded in 2009 in Canada, specializes in autonomous mobile robots for research and industrial applications. The company's focus on providing reliable and adaptable solutions has made it a leader in the field of robotic automation.

2.4.2 Key Innovations

Clearpath Robotics has developed several autonomous robots, including:

- **Otto:** An autonomous mobile robot designed for material handling in warehouses and distribution centers. Otto can navigate without human intervention, optimizing logistics processes.

- **Husky:** A versatile robotic platform used for outdoor and indoor applications, including surveying, mapping, and agricultural tasks.

2.4.3 Impact on Industries

Clearpath's robots have revolutionized material handling in logistics and warehousing. For example, companies utilizing Otto have reported significant reductions in labor costs and increased operational efficiency due to the robot's ability to autonomously transport goods within facilities.

2.5 Case Study: Fanuc

2.5.1 Overview

Fanuc Corporation, established in 1956 in Japan, is a global leader in industrial automation and robotics. The company specializes in CNC systems and a wide range of industrial robots.

2.5.2 Key Innovations

Fanuc's robots include:

- **CR Series:** Collaborative robots designed to work safely alongside humans. The CR Series includes models with various payload capacities, suitable for tasks ranging from assembly to packaging.

- **M-20iA:** An industrial robot known for its precision and speed in handling tasks such as welding, assembly, and material handling.

2.5.3 Impact on Industries

Fanuc's robots have been instrumental in improving manufacturing efficiency. For instance, the use of collaborative robots in assembly lines has enabled manufacturers to enhance productivity while maintaining a safe working environment for human operators.

Conclusion

The case studies presented in this section highlight the innovative approaches and successful implementations of leading robotics companies. Boston Dynamics, Universal Robots, KUKA, Clearpath Robotics, and Fanuc have each made significant contributions to the robotics industry through their unique technologies and applications. These companies not only drive advancements in automation but also shape the future of work by integrating robots into various sectors, enhancing productivity, safety, and efficiency.

3. Competitive Landscape and Market Share

The robotics industry is a dynamic and rapidly evolving sector characterized by significant competition and a diverse range of players, from established manufacturing giants to innovative startups. Understanding the competitive landscape and market share within this industry is crucial for stakeholders seeking to navigate the complexities of robotics. This section explores the key competitors in the robotics market, examines their market positions, and analyzes the factors that contribute to their success or challenges.

The competitive landscape in the robotics industry is shaped by various factors, including technological advancements, regulatory frameworks, and shifting consumer demands. The market is segmented into several categories, such as industrial robots, service robots, and collaborative robots, each with its unique set of competitors. Additionally, the emergence of new technologies, such as artificial intelligence (AI) and the Internet of Things (IoT), has introduced new opportunities and challenges for companies operating in this space.

This chapter will provide a comprehensive overview of the competitive landscape, highlighting the key players, their market shares, and the trends shaping the industry's future.

3.1 Market Segmentation

The robotics industry can be segmented into several key categories:

- **Industrial Robots:** These are primarily used in manufacturing processes, including assembly, welding, painting, and material handling. Major players in this segment include Fanuc, KUKA, ABB, and Yaskawa Electric.

- **Service Robots:** These robots perform tasks in non-manufacturing environments, such as healthcare, hospitality, and domestic applications. Companies like iRobot, Intuitive Surgical, and Universal Robots lead in this segment.

- **Collaborative Robots (Cobots):** Designed to work alongside human operators, cobots are gaining traction in manufacturing and logistics. Universal Robots, Rethink Robotics, and Techman Robot are prominent players in this category.

3.2 Key Players and Market Share

3.2.1 Fanuc Corporation

- **Overview:** Fanuc is one of the largest manufacturers of industrial robots globally, known for its reliability and advanced automation solutions.

- **Market Share:** As of recent estimates, Fanuc holds approximately 20% of the global industrial robot market share, making it a significant player in the industry.

- **Key Products:** The CR Series collaborative robots, M-20iA industrial robots, and a comprehensive range of CNC systems.

3.2.2 KUKA AG

- **Overview:** KUKA, a German company, specializes in industrial robotics and automation technology, serving various sectors, including automotive and healthcare.

- **Market Share:** KUKA holds around 14% of the global market share in industrial robotics.

- **Key Products:** The LBR iiwa collaborative robot, KMR iiwa mobile robot, and a range of industrial automation solutions.

3.2.3 ABB Robotics

- **Overview:** ABB is a leader in industrial automation and robotics, providing solutions for manufacturing, logistics, and service sectors.

- **Market Share:** ABB commands about 10% of the global industrial robotics market.

- **Key Products:** The YuMi collaborative robot and the IRB series of industrial robots.

3.2.4 Universal Robots

- **Overview:** Universal Robots specializes in collaborative robots, making automation accessible to small and medium-sized enterprises (SMEs).

- **Market Share:** Universal Robots has captured around 20% of the collaborative robot market share.

- **Key Products:** The UR3e, UR5e, and UR10e collaborative robots.

3.2.5 iRobot Corporation

- **Overview:** iRobot is a leader in consumer robotics, particularly in the home cleaning sector with its Roomba vacuum series.

- **Market Share:** iRobot holds a significant portion of the consumer robotics market, estimated at 30%.

- **Key Products:** Roomba series and Braava mopping robots.

3.3 Competitive Strategies

The competitive strategies employed by these companies vary significantly based on their target markets and product offerings. Some of the key strategies include:

- **Innovation and R&D:** Companies like Boston Dynamics and KUKA invest heavily in research and development to create cutting-edge robotics solutions that address emerging market needs.

- **Strategic Partnerships:** Collaborations with technology firms, academic institutions, and industry leaders enable companies to enhance their product offerings and expand their market reach. For instance, Universal Robots has partnered with various software companies to develop integrated solutions for different industries.

- **Market Diversification:** Many companies are diversifying their product lines to cater to various sectors. For example, ABB has expanded its offerings from industrial robots to include service robots for healthcare and logistics.

- **Cost Leadership:** Companies like Fanuc and KUKA focus on optimizing production processes to reduce costs and offer competitive pricing, thus attracting a broader customer base.

3.4 Trends Influencing the Competitive Landscape

Several trends are reshaping the competitive landscape of the robotics industry:

- **Increased Demand for Automation:** The push for automation across various sectors is driving the demand for both industrial and service robots. Companies are investing in robotics solutions to improve efficiency and reduce operational costs.

- **Rise of AI and Machine Learning:** The integration of AI and machine learning in robotics is enabling robots to perform complex tasks, enhancing their capabilities and applications.

- **Collaborative Robots on the Rise:** The growing interest in collaborative robots reflects a shift towards automation solutions that can safely work alongside human operators, making them more accessible to SMEs.

- **Sustainability Initiatives:** Robotics companies are increasingly focusing on sustainability, developing energy-efficient robots and solutions that minimize environmental impact.

3.5 Conclusion

The competitive landscape of the robotics industry is characterized by a diverse range of players, each leveraging unique strategies to establish their market presence. Leading companies such as Fanuc, KUKA, ABB, Universal Robots, and iRobot are shaping the future of robotics through innovation, strategic partnerships, and a focus on meeting the evolving demands of various sectors.

As the industry continues to grow, staying informed about market trends and competitors will be essential for stakeholders looking to succeed in this dynamic field.

4. Strategic Partnerships and Collaborations in Robotics

In the rapidly evolving field of robotics, strategic partnerships and collaborations play a crucial role in driving innovation and enhancing competitiveness. These alliances between companies, research institutions, and other stakeholders facilitate the sharing of knowledge, resources, and technology, ultimately leading to the development of advanced robotic solutions. This chapter explores the significance of strategic partnerships in the robotics industry, highlighting key examples, their impact on innovation, and the trends shaping future collaborations.

The robotics landscape is characterized by a diverse array of players, from established manufacturers to startups, all seeking to leverage partnerships to enhance their market positions. Collaborations can take various forms, including joint ventures, research collaborations, technology sharing agreements, and supply chain partnerships. By pooling their expertise, resources, and capabilities, companies can accelerate the development and commercialization of new technologies, improve product offerings, and expand into new markets.

This chapter will delve into the types of strategic partnerships in robotics, case studies of successful collaborations, and the future outlook for partnerships in this dynamic industry.

4.1 Types of Strategic Partnerships in Robotics

4.1.1 Joint Ventures

Joint ventures involve two or more companies coming together to create a new entity, pooling their resources and expertise to pursue specific objectives. This approach allows companies to share risks and rewards while leveraging each other's strengths.

Example: The partnership between Google and ABB to develop advanced robotics solutions for industrial automation showcases how companies can combine their unique capabilities to create innovative products that address market demands.

4.1.2 Research Collaborations

Research collaborations between academic institutions and industry players are essential for advancing robotics technology. These partnerships facilitate the transfer of knowledge and technology, enabling companies to stay at the forefront of innovation.

Example: The collaboration between Carnegie Mellon University and Bosch in the field of robotics research has led to significant advancements in autonomous driving and intelligent robotic systems, enhancing both parties' expertise and product offerings.

4.1.3 Technology Sharing Agreements

Technology sharing agreements enable companies to access each other's technologies and intellectual property, fostering innovation and accelerating product development. This type of partnership is particularly beneficial in fast-paced industries like robotics.

Example: The agreement between Intel and various robotics startups to integrate AI and machine learning capabilities into robotic systems exemplifies how technology sharing can enhance product functionality and performance.

4.1.4 Supply Chain Partnerships

Supply chain partnerships involve collaborations between manufacturers and suppliers to improve efficiency, reduce costs, and enhance product quality. These partnerships are critical in the robotics industry, where precision and reliability are paramount.

Example: The partnership between KUKA and several component manufacturers ensures a steady supply of high-quality parts for their robotic systems, helping to maintain production efficiency and product reliability.

4.2 Case Studies of Successful Partnerships

4.2.1 Toyota and Preferred Networks

Overview: Toyota has partnered with Preferred Networks, a Japanese AI startup, to leverage AI technology for developing autonomous driving systems and robotics applications.

Impact: This collaboration has accelerated Toyota's progress in autonomous vehicle technology, enabling the integration of advanced AI algorithms into their robotics platforms. The partnership highlights how established companies can benefit from the agility and innovation of startups.

4.2.2 Amazon Robotics and Massachusetts Institute of Technology (MIT)

Overview: Amazon Robotics collaborates with MIT to advance research in robotics and automation technologies.

Impact: This partnership has led to innovations in robotic systems used in Amazon's fulfillment centers, enhancing efficiency and reducing operational costs. The collaboration demonstrates the importance of academia-industry partnerships in driving technological advancements.

4.2.3 Siemens and IBM

Overview: Siemens and IBM have formed a strategic partnership to integrate AI and IoT capabilities into Siemens' automation solutions.

Impact: By combining Siemens' expertise in industrial automation with IBM's AI technologies, the partnership has resulted in the development of intelligent manufacturing systems that optimize production processes and enhance decision-making capabilities.

4.3 Benefits of Strategic Partnerships

Strategic partnerships in robotics offer numerous benefits, including:

- **Access to Expertise:** Companies can tap into the specialized knowledge and skills of their partners, enhancing their own capabilities and competitiveness.

- **Shared Risks and Costs:** Collaborations allow companies to share the financial burden of research and development, reducing individual risks associated with new projects.

- **Accelerated Innovation:** By pooling resources and knowledge, companies can accelerate the development and commercialization of new technologies, bringing innovative products to market more quickly.

- **Market Expansion:** Partnerships can help companies enter new markets by leveraging their partners' established customer bases and distribution channels.

4.4 Trends Influencing Partnerships in Robotics

Several trends are shaping the future of strategic partnerships in the robotics industry:

- **Increasing Focus on AI and Machine Learning:** As AI and machine learning technologies become integral to robotics, companies are increasingly partnering with tech firms to incorporate these capabilities into their products.

- **Growth of Collaborative Robots (Cobots):** The rise of collaborative robots has led to partnerships between manufacturers and software developers to create user-friendly interfaces and applications that enhance cobot functionality.

- **Sustainability Initiatives:** Companies are forming partnerships to develop sustainable robotics solutions, focusing on energy efficiency and environmentally friendly materials.

- **Globalization of the Robotics Market:** As robotics companies expand internationally, strategic partnerships with local firms can facilitate market entry and enhance competitiveness.

4.5 Future Outlook

The future of strategic partnerships in robotics is promising, with opportunities for innovation and growth across various sectors. As the industry continues to evolve, companies will need to adapt their partnership strategies to address emerging challenges and leverage new technologies.

Collaborations will likely become more diverse, involving a broader range of stakeholders, including startups, academic institutions, and even governments. As the demand for advanced robotic solutions grows, the importance of strategic partnerships will continue to rise, shaping the future of the robotics industry.

5. Future Competitors and Emerging Startups

The robotics industry is witnessing rapid advancements and transformative changes, driven by technological innovations and the increasing demand for automation across various sectors. As established companies strengthen their foothold, a wave of emerging startups is challenging the status quo, bringing fresh ideas, innovative solutions, and competitive dynamics to the market. This chapter explores the landscape of future competitors and emerging startups in the robotics industry, highlighting key players, their contributions, and the trends shaping this vibrant ecosystem.

Emerging startups often play a pivotal role in driving innovation by introducing novel technologies, products, and business models. These companies are typically agile, adaptable, and more willing to take risks compared to established players, allowing them to respond swiftly to market demands and technological advancements. Furthermore, the convergence of robotics with artificial intelligence (AI), the Internet of Things (IoT), and other disruptive technologies is reshaping the competitive landscape and opening new avenues for growth.

This chapter will examine the characteristics of emerging startups, present notable examples of companies making an impact in the robotics space, analyze the competitive challenges they pose to established firms, and discuss the future outlook for this dynamic sector.

5.1 Characteristics of Emerging Startups in Robotics

Emerging startups in the robotics industry exhibit several defining characteristics:

- **Innovation-Driven:** Startups are often founded on groundbreaking ideas and technologies, focusing on solving specific challenges or addressing unmet needs in the market.

- **Agility and Flexibility:** Smaller organizations can pivot quickly, adapting their business models and product offerings in response to changing market conditions and customer demands.

- **Focus on Niche Markets:** Many startups concentrate on niche applications or industries, allowing them to establish themselves as specialists and gain a competitive advantage.

- **Collaboration with Research Institutions:** Emerging companies frequently partner with academic institutions to leverage cutting-edge research and access advanced technologies.

5.2 Notable Emerging Startups in Robotics

5.2.1 Starship Technologies

Overview: Starship Technologies is a startup specializing in autonomous delivery robots. Founded in 2014 by two Skype co-founders, the company focuses on providing last-mile delivery solutions.

Key Innovations: Starship's delivery robots navigate sidewalks and roads, delivering packages and food directly to customers. The company has partnered with various retailers and food delivery services to streamline delivery operations.

Impact: Starship's robots have gained popularity in urban environments, reducing delivery times and costs while promoting contactless delivery solutions, especially during the COVID-19 pandemic.

5.2.2 Agility Robotics

Overview: Agility Robotics is known for developing bipedal robots designed for various applications, including logistics and human-robot interaction.

Key Innovations: The company's flagship robot, Digit, can navigate complex environments, carry packages, and interact safely with humans. Digit's ability to walk, climb stairs, and perform tasks in dynamic environments sets it apart in the robotics field.

Impact: Agility Robotics aims to enhance efficiency in warehouses and distribution centers, addressing labor shortages and improving productivity.

5.2.3 Cobalt Robotics

Overview: Cobalt Robotics focuses on developing security robots for commercial spaces, combining robotics with artificial intelligence to enhance safety and surveillance.

Key Innovations: Cobalt's robots are equipped with sensors, cameras, and AI capabilities, enabling them to patrol facilities, monitor activities, and respond to incidents in real-time.

Impact: By offering a cost-effective and reliable security solution, Cobalt Robotics addresses the growing need for enhanced security measures in various industries, including retail, healthcare, and corporate settings.

5.2.4 OpenAI Robotics

Overview: OpenAI Robotics is a startup focused on advancing robotics through artificial intelligence and machine learning technologies.

Key Innovations: The company is developing AI-driven robotic systems capable of learning from interactions and improving performance over time. Their research emphasizes the integration of natural language processing into robotic systems, allowing for more intuitive human-robot interactions.

Impact: OpenAI Robotics aims to revolutionize the way humans interact with robots, making them more adaptable and responsive to user needs.

5.3 Competitive Challenges Posed by Startups

Emerging startups present several competitive challenges to established companies in the robotics industry:

- **Disruption of Traditional Business Models:** Startups often introduce innovative business models that disrupt traditional approaches, compelling established firms to adapt or innovate.

- **Increased Innovation Pace:** The agility of startups allows them to bring new technologies and products to market faster than larger corporations, intensifying competition.

- **Talent Acquisition:** Startups are attracting top talent from established companies, further fueling innovation and competition within the industry.

- **Partnerships with Tech Giants:** Many startups collaborate with technology giants to access resources, expertise, and distribution networks, posing a threat to established players that may struggle to compete.

5.4 Trends Shaping the Future of Robotics Startups

Several trends are influencing the growth and development of emerging robotics startups:

- **Rise of Collaborative Robots (Cobots):** The increasing adoption of cobots in industries such as manufacturing and healthcare is creating opportunities for startups to develop specialized applications and solutions.

- **Integration of AI and Machine Learning:** Startups focusing on AI-driven robotics are gaining traction as companies seek smarter, more adaptable robotic solutions that can learn and improve over time.

- **Sustainability Initiatives:** Emerging companies are emphasizing sustainability in their designs and operations, addressing environmental concerns while tapping into the growing market demand for eco-friendly solutions.

- **Healthcare Innovations:** The demand for robotics in healthcare, especially for surgical assistance and rehabilitation, is driving startups to develop innovative solutions that enhance patient care and outcomes.

5.5 Future Outlook for Emerging Startups

The future of emerging startups in the robotics industry looks promising. As technological advancements continue to unfold and industries increasingly adopt automation solutions, startups are well-positioned to capitalize on these trends. The collaborative nature of the robotics ecosystem, characterized by partnerships with established companies, research institutions, and technology providers, will further fuel innovation and growth.

Moreover, as the demand for customized and application-specific robotic solutions rises, startups that focus on niche markets and innovative applications will likely thrive. The ability to adapt to changing market conditions and leverage emerging technologies will be crucial for their success.

In conclusion, the robotics industry is experiencing a significant transformation driven by the emergence of innovative startups. These companies are not only challenging established players but also reshaping the future of robotics through their creative solutions and entrepreneurial spirit.

Chapter 7: Global Markets for Robotics

1. Growth Trends and Market Analysis
2. Key Regions and Countries in Robotics Adoption
3. Industry Applications and Market Segments
4. Consumer Behavior and Trends in Robotics Adoption
5. Economic Impact of Robotics on Global Markets

Chapter 7

Global Markets for Robotics

Introduction

The global robotics market is experiencing unprecedented growth, driven by rapid technological advancements and increasing adoption across various industries. Robotics has evolved from a niche field to a mainstream component of modern manufacturing, healthcare, logistics, and consumer services, fundamentally transforming how businesses operate and deliver value. This chapter delves into the dynamic landscape of global robotics markets, exploring growth trends, key regions, industry applications, consumer behavior, and the economic impact of robotics.

As industries seek to enhance efficiency, reduce operational costs, and improve productivity, the demand for robotic solutions continues to rise. Automation has become a critical strategy for organizations aiming to remain competitive in an increasingly digital and fast-paced economy. In addition, advancements in artificial intelligence, machine learning, and connectivity have propelled the development of smarter, more versatile robotic systems capable of performing complex tasks across various environments.

This chapter will analyze the growth trends shaping the robotics market, identify key regions and countries leading in robotics adoption, examine the diverse industry applications and market segments, assess consumer behavior and adoption trends, and evaluate the overall economic impact of robotics on global markets. By understanding these factors, stakeholders can make informed decisions and strategically position themselves in this rapidly evolving landscape.

In summary, the robotics market presents significant opportunities and challenges, as businesses and consumers alike navigate the implications of automation. The insights provided in this chapter will offer a comprehensive understanding of the current state and future prospects of the global robotics market.

1. Growth Trends and Market Analysis

The robotics industry is experiencing an unprecedented phase of growth, fueled by advancements in technology, increasing automation across various sectors, and the demand for innovative solutions to enhance productivity and efficiency. This chapter delves into the key growth trends shaping the robotics market, analyzes the factors driving this growth, and provides a comprehensive market analysis to identify opportunities and challenges faced by stakeholders in this dynamic field.

1.1 Current Market Size and Forecast

The global robotics market was valued at approximately **$39.8 billion in 2021** and is projected to reach around **$102.5 billion by 2028**, growing at a compound annual growth rate (CAGR) of approximately **14.5%** from 2022 to 2028. This growth is primarily driven by the increasing adoption of automation technologies in manufacturing, healthcare, logistics, and consumer applications.

Example:

For example, the manufacturing sector is one of the largest consumers of robotics technology. Companies like **Fanuc, ABB, and KUKA** have significantly increased their investments in robotic systems, facilitating enhanced productivity and precision in production processes.

1.2 Key Growth Drivers

Several key factors are propelling the growth of the robotics market:

1.2.1 Technological Advancements

Innovations in robotics technology, including artificial intelligence (AI), machine learning, computer vision, and sensor technologies, have greatly enhanced the capabilities of robots. These advancements enable robots to perform more complex tasks autonomously and efficiently.

1.2.2 Labor Shortages and Rising Labor Costs

Many industries are facing labor shortages, particularly in sectors such as manufacturing and healthcare. As a result, organizations are increasingly turning to robotics to automate repetitive and labor-intensive tasks, which helps mitigate the impact of labor shortages and rising wage demands.

1.2.3 Increased Focus on Safety and Efficiency

The COVID-19 pandemic has accelerated the adoption of robotics, particularly in healthcare and logistics, as businesses seek to reduce human contact and ensure operational efficiency. Robots are being utilized for disinfection, telepresence, and remote monitoring, highlighting their importance in maintaining health and safety standards.

1.3 Market Segmentation

The robotics market can be segmented based on application, type, and region:

1.3.1 By Application

- **Industrial Robotics**: This segment includes robots used in manufacturing processes, such as assembly, welding, and packaging. Industrial robots are essential for automating tasks that require precision and speed.

- **Service Robotics**: Service robots are increasingly used in healthcare (e.g., surgical robots), hospitality, agriculture, and cleaning applications. They enhance service delivery and operational efficiency in various environments.

- **Collaborative Robotics**: Cobots are designed to work alongside humans, improving workplace safety and efficiency. These robots are gaining traction in manufacturing environments where human-robot collaboration is essential.

1.3.2 By Type

- **Autonomous Robots**: These robots operate independently using advanced AI and navigation systems. Examples include autonomous mobile robots (AMRs) used in warehouses for material handling.

- **Semi-Autonomous Robots**: These require some level of human control or intervention but can perform specific tasks independently.

1.4 Regional Analysis

The global robotics market demonstrates diverse growth trends across various regions:

1.4.1 North America

North America remains a leader in robotics adoption, driven by advanced manufacturing technologies and a robust presence of major robotics manufacturers. The U.S. market is particularly strong in industrial robotics, with companies such as **Rockwell Automation** and **iRobot** contributing to growth.

1.4.2 Europe

Europe is witnessing rapid growth in service robotics, especially in healthcare and logistics. Countries like **Germany**, **France**, and **the UK** are at the forefront of robotics innovation, with significant government initiatives supporting research and development.

1.4.3 Asia-Pacific

The Asia-Pacific region is experiencing the fastest growth in the robotics market, fueled by increasing labor costs and rising automation in manufacturing. **China** is the largest market for industrial robots globally, with major manufacturers like **Siasun** and **Estun Automation** leading the way.

1.5 Challenges and Barriers to Growth

Despite the positive growth trends, the robotics market faces several challenges:

1.5.1 High Initial Costs

The initial investment required for robotic systems can be a barrier for small and medium-sized enterprises (SMEs). Although the long-term savings and efficiency gains are significant, the upfront costs remain a concern.

1.5.2 Integration Complexities

Integrating robotics into existing workflows can be complex and require substantial changes in processes and employee training. Organizations may encounter resistance from employees concerned about job displacement or operational changes.

1.5.3 Regulatory and Ethical Concerns

As robotics technology evolves, regulatory and ethical issues surrounding safety, privacy, and job displacement arise. Policymakers must establish clear guidelines to address these concerns while fostering a supportive environment for robotics innovation.

Conclusion

In conclusion, the robotics market is poised for significant growth, driven by technological advancements, labor dynamics, and increasing automation demand across industries. While opportunities abound, stakeholders must navigate challenges such as initial costs and integration complexities. Understanding these growth trends and market dynamics is essential for organizations looking to leverage the transformative potential of robotics.

2. Key Regions and Countries in Robotics Adoption

The robotics industry is witnessing an exponential growth trajectory across the globe, driven by advancements in technology and increasing adoption across various sectors. Different regions exhibit unique trends and dynamics in robotics adoption, influenced by factors such as economic development, technological infrastructure, labor markets, and government policies. This chapter aims to explore the key regions and countries leading in robotics adoption, analyzing their respective market characteristics, challenges, and opportunities.

2.1 North America

2.1.1 Overview

North America, particularly the United States, is at the forefront of robotics adoption, spearheaded by technological advancements and significant investments in automation. The region is home to many leading robotics companies and research institutions, fostering an environment conducive to innovation.

2.1.2 Market Characteristics

- **Market Size**: The North American robotics market was valued at approximately **$12.6 billion in 2021** and is expected to grow significantly, driven by increasing automation in manufacturing and healthcare sectors.

- **Key Players**: Prominent robotics manufacturers include **Rockwell Automation, iRobot, KUKA**, and **ABB**.

- **Government Initiatives**: Various government initiatives aim to promote robotics and automation, such as the **National Robotics Initiative (NRI)**, which encourages collaboration between government, academia, and industry.

2.1.3 Key Applications

- **Manufacturing**: North America is a leader in industrial robotics, with automation playing a crucial role in enhancing productivity and precision in manufacturing processes.

- **Healthcare**: Surgical robots and telepresence robots are gaining traction in hospitals and clinics, improving patient outcomes and operational efficiency.

2.1.4 Challenges

- **High Initial Costs**: The high costs associated with robotic systems can deter smaller enterprises from adopting these technologies.

- **Labor Concerns**: There are ongoing concerns about job displacement due to automation, prompting discussions around workforce retraining.

2.2 Europe

2.2.1 Overview

Europe is a major player in the global robotics market, with a strong emphasis on innovation and research. The region benefits from a well-established manufacturing base and a growing demand for service robotics.

2.2.2 Market Characteristics

- **Market Size**: The European robotics market is projected to reach **$23 billion by 2028**, driven by advancements in both industrial and service robotics.

- **Key Players**: Major manufacturers include **Siemens**, **KUKA**, and **FANUC**.

- **Government Policies**: The European Union has implemented various funding programs to support robotics research and innovation, such as the **Horizon 2020** program.

2.2.3 Key Applications

- **Industrial Robotics**: Germany, known as the "Manufacturing Hub of Europe," leads in industrial automation, with a significant concentration of robotics companies.

- **Service Robotics**: Countries like France and the Netherlands are investing heavily in healthcare robotics, particularly in elder care and rehabilitation.

2.2.4 Challenges

- **Regulatory Barriers**: Different countries have varying regulations regarding the use of robotics, creating challenges for manufacturers operating across borders.

- **Skill Gaps**: There is a notable skills gap in the workforce, necessitating retraining and education to meet the demands of a robotic workforce.

2.3 Asia-Pacific

2.3.1 Overview

The Asia-Pacific region is experiencing the fastest growth in robotics adoption, driven by rapid industrialization and increasing labor costs. Countries like China, Japan, and South Korea are leading the way in terms of innovation and implementation.

2.3.2 Market Characteristics

- **Market Size**: The Asia-Pacific robotics market was valued at around **$19.5 billion in 2021** and is expected to witness robust growth, particularly in industrial and collaborative robotics.

- **Key Players**: Notable companies include **Fanuc, Yaskawa Electric**, and **Kawasaki Robotics**.

- **Government Support**: Governments in the region are implementing initiatives to promote robotics and automation, with China investing heavily in becoming a global leader in robotics by 2025.

2.3.3 Key Applications

- **Manufacturing**: China is the largest market for industrial robots globally, focusing on automating production lines across various industries, including electronics and automotive.

- **Logistics and Warehousing**: Companies like **Alibaba** and **JD.com** are utilizing robotics for warehouse automation and last-mile delivery, enhancing operational efficiency.

2.3.4 Challenges

- **Quality Control**: As the market grows, ensuring the quality and reliability of robotic systems becomes increasingly critical.

- **Intellectual Property Concerns**: The rapid pace of innovation raises concerns about intellectual property protection and infringement.

2.4 Latin America

2.4.1 Overview

Latin America is an emerging market for robotics, with increasing interest in automation from various sectors, particularly manufacturing and agriculture. While adoption is currently lower than in North America, Europe, or Asia-Pacific, growth potential exists.

2.4.2 Market Characteristics

- **Market Size**: The Latin American robotics market is valued at approximately **$2 billion**, with expected growth driven by rising automation trends in industries.

- **Key Players**: Local manufacturers are beginning to emerge, alongside global companies expanding their presence in the region.

2.4.3 Key Applications

- **Manufacturing**: Brazilian industries are increasingly adopting robotics to enhance productivity and competitiveness.

- **Agricultural Robotics**: Countries like Argentina and Brazil are exploring the use of robotics in agriculture to optimize production and reduce labor costs.

2.4.4 Challenges

- **Economic Instability**: Economic fluctuations can impact investment in robotics, creating uncertainties in the market.

- **Lack of Infrastructure**: Limited technological infrastructure in some areas can hinder the adoption of advanced robotics.

2.5 Middle East and Africa

2.5.1 Overview

The Middle East and Africa (MEA) represent a nascent but growing market for robotics, with increasing investment in automation across various sectors. The region is focused on diversifying economies and enhancing technological capabilities.

2.5.2 Market Characteristics

*   **Market Size**: The MEA robotics market is estimated to be around **$1 billion**, with potential for growth in industries like oil and gas, healthcare, and logistics.

*   **Key Players**: International robotics companies are entering the market, supported by local initiatives promoting technology adoption.

2.5.3 Key Applications

*   **Healthcare Robotics**: Countries like the UAE are investing in robotic technologies for healthcare, focusing on surgical robots and telemedicine.

*   **Oil and Gas**: Robotics is increasingly being utilized for inspection and maintenance in the oil and gas sector, enhancing safety and efficiency.

2.5.4 Challenges

*   **Limited Awareness**: Awareness and understanding of robotics technology remain low in many regions, hindering adoption.

*   **Regulatory Frameworks**: Developing comprehensive regulatory frameworks for robotics and automation is essential to foster growth.

Conclusion

In summary, robotics adoption is progressing at different rates across key regions, driven by various economic, technological, and social factors. North America and Europe lead in terms of market maturity and technological advancement, while the Asia-Pacific region is rapidly catching up, particularly in manufacturing and logistics applications. Emerging markets in Latin America and the MEA region present unique challenges and opportunities, with significant potential for growth as industries increasingly recognize the value of robotics in enhancing efficiency and productivity.

3. Industry Applications and Market Segments

The rapid evolution of robotics technology has led to its adoption across various industries, transforming traditional practices and creating new opportunities. Robotics applications are diverse, ranging from manufacturing and healthcare to agriculture and logistics. Each sector has unique requirements and challenges that robotics can address, leading to increased efficiency, productivity, and safety. This chapter will explore the key industry applications of robotics, identifying market segments, and examining how different sectors are leveraging robotic technologies to enhance operations.

3.1 Robotics in Manufacturing

3.1.1 Overview

Manufacturing is one of the most significant sectors adopting robotics technology. The integration of robots in production lines has revolutionized the way products are made, enabling higher precision and efficiency.

3.1.2 Types of Robotics Used

- **Industrial Robots**: These include robotic arms used for welding, painting, assembly, and material handling. For example, **FANUC** and **ABB** provide robots that automate tasks in automotive manufacturing.

- **Collaborative Robots (Cobots)**: Cobots work alongside human operators, enhancing productivity without replacing the human workforce. Companies like **Universal Robots** are at the forefront of this technology.

3.1.3 Examples

- **Automotive Industry**: Companies like **Tesla** and **Ford** use robots extensively on their assembly lines for tasks such as welding and painting, achieving higher throughput and reduced error rates.

- **Electronics Manufacturing**: Firms like **Apple** and **Samsung** utilize precision robots for assembly and inspection processes, ensuring high quality in their products.

3.1.4 Market Trends

- **Increased Automation**: There is a growing trend towards fully automated factories, known as "lights-out" manufacturing, where robots operate without human intervention.

- **Customization**: Advances in robotics are enabling more customized production runs, responding to changing consumer demands.

3.2 Robotics in Healthcare

3.2.1 Overview

The healthcare sector has witnessed a significant transformation with the introduction of robotics, improving patient outcomes and enhancing the efficiency of medical procedures.

3.2.2 Types of Robotics Used

- **Surgical Robots**: These allow surgeons to perform minimally invasive procedures with precision. The **da Vinci Surgical System** is a leading example, enabling complex surgeries with smaller incisions.

- **Rehabilitation Robots**: Devices like exoskeletons assist patients in regaining mobility after injuries or surgeries.

3.2.3 Examples

- **Surgical Applications**: The **da Vinci Surgical System** has been used in thousands of procedures worldwide, improving recovery times and reducing complications.

- **Physical Therapy**: The **EksoGT** exoskeleton helps patients with lower extremity paralysis regain movement, demonstrating the potential of robotics in rehabilitation.

3.2.4 Market Trends

- **Telemedicine**: The rise of telemedicine has increased the demand for robotic systems that facilitate remote surgeries and consultations.

- **Aging Population**: As the global population ages, the demand for robotic solutions in elder care and rehabilitation is expected to rise.

3.3 Robotics in Logistics and Supply Chain

3.3.1 Overview

The logistics and supply chain industry is increasingly relying on robotics to streamline operations, reduce costs, and improve delivery times.

3.3.2 Types of Robotics Used

- **Automated Guided Vehicles (AGVs)**: These robots transport materials and products within warehouses and distribution centers, minimizing the need for manual labor.

- **Drones**: Used for inventory management and delivery, drones are becoming an integral part of logistics operations.

3.3.3 Examples

- **Warehouse Automation**: Companies like **Amazon** employ Kiva robots to move products around warehouses, significantly speeding up order fulfillment.

- **Delivery Drones**: **Wing**, a subsidiary of Alphabet, has successfully conducted drone deliveries in select markets, showcasing the potential for faster last-mile delivery.

3.3.4 Market Trends

- **E-commerce Growth**: The surge in e-commerce has driven the adoption of robotic systems to meet increased demand for rapid order fulfillment.

- **Smart Warehousing**: The trend toward smart warehouses integrates robotics with IoT technologies for real-time inventory management and predictive analytics.

3.4 Robotics in Agriculture

3.4.1 Overview

The agricultural sector is increasingly adopting robotics to enhance productivity, reduce labor costs, and improve crop management practices.

3.4.2 Types of Robotics Used

- **Autonomous Tractors**: These self-driving vehicles perform tasks such as planting, harvesting, and tilling without human intervention.

- **Drones**: Used for crop monitoring, pest control, and aerial imaging, drones are revolutionizing precision agriculture.

3.4.3 Examples

- **Autonomous Tractors**: Companies like **John Deere** are developing autonomous tractors that can operate continuously, optimizing planting and harvesting processes.

- **Drone Technology**: **DJI** drones are widely used for aerial crop monitoring, helping farmers assess crop health and make informed decisions.

3.4.4 Market Trends

- **Sustainability**: The shift toward sustainable farming practices is driving the adoption of robotic solutions that reduce chemical use and improve resource management.

- **Labor Shortages**: Robotics provides a solution to labor shortages in agriculture, enabling farmers to maintain productivity levels.

3.5 Robotics in Retail

3.5.1 Overview

Robotics is beginning to play a role in the retail sector, enhancing customer experiences and streamlining operations.

3.5.2 Types of Robotics Used

- **Service Robots**: Robots that assist customers in stores, providing information and helping with navigation.

- **Inventory Robots**: These robots automate inventory management, ensuring that stock levels are maintained accurately.

3.5.3 Examples

- **Service Robots**: Companies like **SoftBank Robotics** offer robots like **Pepper**, which interact with customers and provide assistance in retail environments.

- **Inventory Management**: **Walmart** uses robots for scanning shelves to monitor stock levels and identify items that need restocking.

3.5.4 Market Trends

- **Personalization**: Retailers are using robotics to create personalized shopping experiences, leveraging data to tailor interactions with customers.

- **Omni-channel Retailing**: Robotics supports the integration of online and offline shopping experiences, improving fulfillment and customer service.

Conclusion

Robotics is making significant inroads across various industries, each benefiting from enhanced efficiency, productivity, and safety. As technology continues to evolve, the applications of robotics are likely to expand further, creating new opportunities and challenges. Understanding these industry applications and market segments is crucial for stakeholders looking to navigate the changing landscape of robotics and capitalize on emerging trends.

4. Consumer Behavior and Trends in Robotics Adoption

The rapid advancement of robotics technology has significantly influenced consumer behavior, transforming the way individuals interact with robots in their daily lives. As robotics systems become more sophisticated and accessible, understanding the factors driving consumer adoption is crucial for businesses and manufacturers. This section will explore the dynamics of consumer behavior related to robotics, including motivations for adoption, barriers to entry, and trends shaping the market. By analyzing real-world examples and case studies, we can gain insights into how consumers perceive robotics and the future implications for this emerging market.

4.1 Factors Influencing Consumer Adoption of Robotics

4.1.1 Technological Advancements

As robotics technology evolves, consumers are increasingly drawn to the capabilities offered by advanced robotic systems. Innovations in artificial intelligence, machine learning, and sensor technology enhance the functionality and usability of robots, making them more appealing to consumers.

- **Example**: **Robot Vacuum Cleaners**: Devices like the **Roomba** utilize advanced sensors and AI algorithms to navigate homes autonomously, appealing to consumers seeking convenience and efficiency in household chores.

4.1.2 Cost Considerations

Price plays a critical role in consumer adoption. While some consumers are willing to invest in high-end robotic systems, others may be deterred by the initial costs. The price-to-value ratio is crucial in determining whether consumers perceive a robotic product as worth the investment.

- **Example**: High-end surgical robots can cost millions of dollars, making them accessible primarily to hospitals and large healthcare facilities, while lower-cost consumer robots are marketed towards individual users.

4.1.3 Social Influence and Peer Recommendations

Social factors, including peer recommendations, reviews, and the influence of social media, significantly impact consumer decisions. Positive testimonials and endorsements from early adopters can drive interest and acceptance among potential customers.

- **Example**: Platforms like **YouTube** feature numerous reviews and demonstrations of consumer robots, such as smart assistants (e.g., **Amazon Echo**) and home security robots (e.g., **Ring**), influencing consumer perceptions and encouraging purchases.

4.1.4 User Experience and Design

The design and user experience of robotic systems significantly affect consumer acceptance. Intuitive interfaces, aesthetic appeal, and user-friendly features enhance the likelihood of adoption.

- **Example**: Robots like **Sony's Aibo** robotic dog have gained popularity due to their engaging design and interactive features, providing an enjoyable experience for consumers.

4.2 Barriers to Robotics Adoption

4.2.1 Lack of Awareness and Understanding

Many consumers may not fully understand the benefits of robotics or how these systems can enhance their lives. Misconceptions and limited knowledge can hinder adoption.

- **Example**: Some individuals may perceive robots as complex or intimidating, leading to reluctance in using robotic systems in their homes or workplaces.

4.2.2 Privacy and Security Concerns

With the increased use of robotics comes concerns about privacy and data security. Consumers are cautious about how their personal information is used and whether robotic systems can be hacked or misused.

- **Example**: Concerns regarding surveillance capabilities in home security robots have led some consumers to hesitate in adopting such technologies.

4.2.3 Reliability and Trust Issues

Consumers need to trust that robotic systems will perform as expected and not malfunction. Reliability is crucial in establishing consumer confidence in robotics.

- **Example**: Early robotic vacuum models faced criticism for poor navigation and cleaning performance, which damaged consumer trust in the category.

4.3 Trends in Robotics Adoption

4.3.1 Increasing Integration of AI

The integration of artificial intelligence in robotic systems is a significant trend influencing consumer behavior. AI enhances robots' capabilities, allowing for more personalized and efficient interactions.

- **Example**: Virtual assistants like **Google Assistant** and **Amazon Alexa** are becoming integral to smart home systems, demonstrating how AI can enhance the functionality of consumer robots.

4.3.2 Growth in Smart Home Technologies

As smart home technologies become more prevalent, consumers are increasingly adopting robotics as part of their connected ecosystems. Robotics complements other smart devices, creating seamless automation in the home.

- **Example**: Consumers often pair robotic vacuum cleaners with smart home platforms (e.g., **Google Home**, **Amazon Alexa**) to schedule cleaning tasks through voice commands.

4.3.3 Rising Interest in Personal and Companion Robots

There is a growing trend towards personal and companion robots, reflecting consumer desires for companionship and social interaction. Robots designed for emotional engagement are gaining traction in the market.

- **Example**: Products like **Cozmo**, a small robot designed to interact with users, appeal to consumers seeking both entertainment and companionship.

4.4 Case Studies of Consumer Robotics Adoption

4.4.1 Roomba by iRobot

Roomba, a robotic vacuum cleaner, revolutionized the home cleaning market. iRobot leveraged consumer insights to design a product that meets the needs of busy households. The success of Roomba can be attributed to effective marketing strategies, positive user experiences, and a focus on reliability.

- **Key Takeaways**: The importance of user feedback in product development and the role of marketing in driving consumer awareness.

4.4.2 Paro Therapeutic Robot

Paro is a therapeutic robot designed to provide comfort and companionship to patients in healthcare settings. Its success highlights the potential for robotics in improving quality of life for vulnerable populations.

- **Key Takeaways**: Understanding the specific needs of target consumers is crucial for successful product adoption, particularly in specialized markets like healthcare.

Conclusion

Understanding consumer behavior and the trends influencing robotics adoption is vital for manufacturers and stakeholders in the robotics industry. By addressing the factors that drive interest and overcoming barriers to entry, companies can successfully navigate the evolving landscape of consumer robotics. As technology continues to advance and consumer preferences shift, the robotics market will likely witness significant growth and transformation in the coming years.

5. Economic Impact of Robotics on Global Markets

The integration of robotics into various sectors has ushered in transformative changes to global economies. Robotics technology enhances productivity, efficiency, and innovation across industries, impacting job markets, economic growth, and the overall dynamics of commerce. This section delves into the economic implications of robotics on global markets, examining its effects on productivity, employment, and economic structures. Through real-world examples and case studies, we will explore how robotics is reshaping industries and influencing economic policies.

5.1 Overview of the Economic Impact of Robotics

Robotics technology contributes significantly to economic growth through enhanced productivity and efficiency. By automating repetitive tasks, businesses can streamline operations, reduce costs, and increase output, resulting in a more robust economic environment.

5.1.1 Increased Productivity

Robots can operate continuously without fatigue, leading to higher levels of productivity. In manufacturing, for instance, robots can perform tasks at speeds and precision levels unattainable by human workers.

- **Example**: In automotive manufacturing, companies like **Ford** and **Toyota** have integrated robotic assembly lines, resulting in faster production times and reduced labor costs. This integration has led to higher output levels and improved quality in vehicle manufacturing.

5.1.2 Cost Reduction

The deployment of robotics can significantly lower operational costs. By automating tasks, companies can reduce labor expenses and minimize errors associated with manual work.

- **Example**: **Amazon** employs robotic systems in its warehouses, optimizing inventory management and order fulfillment processes. The use of robots has decreased operational costs and enhanced delivery efficiency, allowing Amazon to maintain its competitive edge.

5.2 Robotics and Employment Dynamics

The rise of robotics has sparked debates about its impact on employment. While automation can displace certain jobs, it can also create new opportunities and enhance job quality in various sectors.

5.2.1 Job Displacement vs. Job Creation

Robotics technology may lead to job displacement in some industries, particularly in roles that involve repetitive or low-skilled tasks. However, it also generates demand for skilled workers in robotics design, maintenance, and programming.

- **Example**: The introduction of robots in manufacturing has led to a decrease in demand for assembly line workers while simultaneously increasing the need for robotics engineers and technicians.

5.2.2 Upskilling and Reskilling Workforce

As the robotics landscape evolves, there is an increasing emphasis on upskilling and reskilling the workforce. Educational institutions and businesses must collaborate to provide training programs that equip workers with the necessary skills to thrive in an automated environment.

- **Example**: Many companies, including **Siemens**, have initiated training programs to help employees adapt to new technologies and understand how to work alongside robots effectively.

5.3 Robotics and Economic Growth

The economic growth driven by robotics is evident in various sectors, from manufacturing to healthcare. By enhancing productivity and efficiency, robotics contributes to the overall growth of economies worldwide.

5.3.1 Robotics in Manufacturing

The manufacturing sector has witnessed significant transformations due to robotics. Automation increases production capacity and efficiency, enabling companies to scale operations and enter new markets.

- **Example**: The use of robotics in electronics manufacturing, such as **Apple's** assembly lines, has allowed for rapid product development and increased output, contributing to the company's sustained economic growth.

5.3.2 Robotics in Healthcare

In the healthcare sector, robotics enhances patient care, streamlining procedures and improving outcomes. Surgical robots, for instance, allow for minimally invasive surgeries, resulting in shorter recovery times and reduced hospital stays.

- **Example**: The **da Vinci Surgical System** has transformed surgical procedures, leading to better patient outcomes and efficiency in healthcare delivery.

5.4 Challenges and Economic Considerations

While the economic impact of robotics is largely positive, several challenges must be addressed to maximize benefits and minimize adverse effects.

5.4.1 Initial Investment Costs

The high initial costs of implementing robotic systems can deter small and medium-sized enterprises (SMEs) from adopting automation technologies. This barrier must be addressed to ensure widespread adoption across industries.

- **Example**: SMEs in the manufacturing sector may struggle to afford the latest robotic technologies, leading to a disparity in competitiveness compared to larger corporations.

5.4.2 Regulatory and Ethical Considerations

As robotics technology advances, regulatory and ethical considerations must be taken into account. Policymakers need to establish guidelines to ensure the safe and ethical use of robotics in various sectors.

- **Example**: Governments must navigate issues related to job displacement, privacy concerns, and the ethical implications of deploying robots in sensitive environments, such as healthcare and law enforcement.

5.5 Case Studies on Economic Impact of Robotics

5.5.1 South Korea: A Leader in Robotics Adoption

South Korea has emerged as a global leader in robotics adoption, with a strong emphasis on integrating robotics into its manufacturing sector. The government's proactive policies and investments in robotics technology have led to increased productivity and economic growth.

- **Key Takeaways**: South Korea's focus on robotics has positioned it as a competitive player in the global market, demonstrating the potential economic benefits of embracing automation.

5.5.2 Japan: Robotics in Elderly Care

Japan faces a significant challenge with an aging population, leading to increased demand for elderly care services. The country has turned to robotics to address this issue, deploying robots for caregiving and assistance.

- **Key Takeaways**: Japan's investment in robotics for elderly care has not only improved the quality of life for seniors but also contributed to economic growth by alleviating workforce shortages in the caregiving sector.

Conclusion

The economic impact of robotics on global markets is profound, influencing productivity, employment dynamics, and overall economic growth. While challenges exist, the potential benefits of robotics in enhancing efficiency and creating new opportunities far outweigh the drawbacks. As industries continue to embrace automation, understanding the economic implications of robotics will be crucial for policymakers, businesses, and the workforce to navigate this transformative landscape effectively.

Chapter 8: Regulatory and Ethical Framework

1. Overview of Robotics Regulations Globally
2. Ethical Considerations in Robotics Development and Deployment
3. Impact of Legislation on Robotics Adoption
4. Privacy Concerns and Data Security in Robotics
5. Future Directions for Robotics Regulation and Ethics

Chapter 8

Regulatory and Ethical Framework

Introduction

As robotics technology continues to evolve and integrate into various sectors, the need for a comprehensive regulatory and ethical framework becomes increasingly crucial. The transformative potential of robotics raises significant questions regarding safety, accountability, privacy, and the moral implications of automation in everyday life. This chapter explores the complex landscape of robotics regulations globally, highlighting the diverse approaches adopted by different countries and regions.

Furthermore, it delves into the ethical considerations that accompany the development and deployment of robotic systems, examining issues such as decision-making, bias, and the impact on human employment. The interplay between legislation and robotics adoption is also analyzed, shedding light on how laws shape the pace and extent of technological integration across industries.

As robotics permeates our lives, concerns about privacy and data security become paramount. This chapter will discuss the challenges associated with safeguarding sensitive information in an increasingly automated world. Finally, we will consider future directions for robotics regulation and ethics, exploring how policymakers, industry leaders, and ethicists can collaborate to create a framework that fosters innovation while protecting societal interests. Through this exploration, we aim to establish a foundational understanding of the regulatory and ethical dimensions of robotics, preparing stakeholders for the challenges and opportunities that lie ahead.

1. Overview of Robotics Regulations Globally

The rapid advancement of robotics technology has sparked significant interest across various sectors, including healthcare, manufacturing, logistics, and personal assistance. As robots become integral to everyday life and industry, the need for a robust regulatory framework to ensure their safe and ethical deployment has never been more critical. This section provides an overview of robotics regulations globally, examining the current landscape, the challenges faced, and the future directions for regulation.

1.1 The Need for Regulation

The increasing reliance on robots brings both opportunities and challenges. While robotics can enhance productivity, safety, and efficiency, it also raises concerns regarding job displacement, safety standards, accountability, and ethical implications. Regulation aims to address these concerns by setting clear guidelines and standards for the design, manufacturing, and deployment of robotic systems.

1.2 Global Regulatory Landscape

1.2.1 North America

In North America, regulatory frameworks for robotics are evolving. The United States has a decentralized approach, with various agencies involved in regulating different aspects of robotics. The Occupational Safety and Health Administration (OSHA) provides guidelines to ensure workplace safety involving robotics, while the National

Highway Traffic Safety Administration (NHTSA) oversees autonomous vehicles.

For example, in 2020, the U.S. Department of Transportation issued a comprehensive framework for autonomous vehicle testing and deployment, which emphasized safety, innovation, and accountability. In Canada, the government has also introduced guidelines for the safe use of robots in industrial settings, emphasizing risk assessment and management.

1.2.2 Europe

Europe has been proactive in establishing regulations for robotics. The European Commission proposed the "European strategy on robotics" in 2018, which aims to create a unified regulatory framework across member states. The EU's General Data Protection Regulation (GDPR) also impacts robotics, especially concerning data privacy and protection in systems that use personal data.

One notable initiative is the European Union's Robotics and Artificial Intelligence (AI) Act, which seeks to categorize robots based on their level of risk and establish specific requirements for high-risk categories. For instance, medical robots used in surgeries would require rigorous testing and certification before deployment.

1.2.3 Asia

In Asia, countries like Japan and South Korea have developed comprehensive robotics strategies. Japan has long been a leader in robotics, with a focus on industrial automation and personal assistance robots. The Japanese government has implemented policies to promote robotics while ensuring safety and standards through organizations like the Japan Industrial Robotics Association (JARA).

South Korea has also prioritized robotics in its national agenda, with the "Korea Robot Industry Development Plan" focusing on innovation, workforce development, and safety regulations. In 2020, South Korea introduced a regulatory framework to promote the safe integration of drones into its airspace, reflecting the growing importance of aerial robotics.

1.3 Key Challenges in Robotics Regulation

1.3.1 Rapid Technological Advancement

One of the significant challenges in regulating robotics is the rapid pace of technological advancement. Regulators often struggle to keep up with innovations, leading to outdated regulations that may not effectively address current technologies. This can hinder innovation and create uncertainty in the industry.

1.3.2 Lack of Standardization

The absence of global standards for robotics creates inconsistencies in regulations across countries. Different countries may have varying safety requirements, testing protocols, and liability frameworks, complicating international trade and collaboration in the robotics industry.

1.3.3 Ethical Considerations

Ethical concerns surrounding robotics, such as decision-making in autonomous systems, biases in algorithms, and the potential for job displacement, pose additional challenges for regulators. Addressing these ethical considerations requires collaboration between technologists, ethicists, and policymakers to create guidelines that promote responsible development and deployment.

1.4 Future Directions for Robotics Regulation

1.4.1 International Collaboration

To address the challenges of robotics regulation effectively, international collaboration is essential. Organizations like the International Organization for Standardization (ISO) and the International Electrotechnical Commission (IEC) play a crucial role in developing global standards that can facilitate safe and harmonized robotics deployment worldwide.

1.4.2 Adaptive Regulatory Frameworks

Regulators need to adopt adaptive frameworks that can evolve alongside technological advancements. This includes continuous monitoring and assessment of emerging technologies, allowing for timely updates to regulations and standards.

1.4.3 Emphasizing Ethical Guidelines

Incorporating ethical guidelines into the regulatory framework is crucial for fostering public trust in robotics. Engaging stakeholders, including industry experts, ethicists, and the public, in discussions about ethical implications can lead to more comprehensive regulations that address societal concerns.

Conclusion

The global regulatory landscape for robotics is dynamic and continues to evolve in response to technological advancements and societal needs. While significant progress has been made in establishing frameworks, challenges such as rapid innovation, standardization, and ethical considerations remain. Moving forward, a collaborative and adaptive approach to regulation will be essential to harness the benefits of robotics while ensuring safety, accountability, and ethical responsibility.

2. Ethical Considerations in Robotics Development and Deployment

The integration of robotics into various sectors has the potential to revolutionize industries and improve quality of life. However, as robots become increasingly autonomous and capable of making decisions, ethical considerations in their development and deployment have gained prominence. This section explores the ethical dilemmas and considerations associated with robotics, emphasizing the importance of responsible innovation. It will examine issues such as accountability, privacy, bias, and the implications of human-robot interaction. By addressing these ethical challenges, stakeholders can work towards a future where robotics benefits society while minimizing harm.

2.1 The Importance of Ethics in Robotics

Ethics in robotics involves evaluating the moral implications of designing and deploying robotic systems. As robots take on roles traditionally held by humans, their decision-making processes can have significant consequences. Ethical considerations help ensure that these systems align with societal values and promote human welfare.

2.1.1 Historical Context

Historically, the development of robotics has focused primarily on functionality and efficiency, often neglecting ethical implications. Early robots were designed for specific tasks in controlled environments, such as manufacturing. However, as robotics technology advanced and began to influence everyday life, the need for ethical frameworks became evident.

2.1.2 Current Trends

Today, the field of robotics is characterized by increased autonomy and decision-making capabilities. Robots are now utilized in healthcare, transportation, and even companionship. As these technologies become more integrated into society, ethical considerations must be at the forefront of their development.

2.2 Key Ethical Issues in Robotics

2.2.1 Accountability and Responsibility

One of the most pressing ethical issues in robotics is accountability. When a robot makes a decision that leads to harm or adverse outcomes, questions arise about who is responsible: the developer, the user, or the robot itself?

2.2.1.1 Case Study: Autonomous Vehicles

Autonomous vehicles provide a relevant example of accountability challenges. In the event of an accident involving an autonomous vehicle, determining liability can be complex. Legal frameworks must evolve to address questions about manufacturer responsibility, software integrity, and driver oversight.

2.2.2 Privacy Concerns

As robots become increasingly integrated into personal and professional environments, they often collect vast amounts of data. This raises significant privacy concerns regarding how data is used, stored, and shared.

2.2.2.1 Example: Social Robots

Social robots, such as those used in homes or healthcare settings, may collect sensitive information about individuals. Ethical considerations must ensure that user privacy is respected and that data is used responsibly. Developers should implement robust data protection measures to safeguard user information.

2.2.3 Bias and Fairness

Robotic systems can inadvertently perpetuate or amplify biases present in their training data. Ensuring fairness in robotics development is crucial to prevent discrimination and promote equitable outcomes.

2.2.3.1 Case Study: AI in Hiring

In the context of hiring, algorithms used by robotic systems to screen candidates can reflect biases present in historical data. For instance, if an algorithm is trained on data that predominantly features successful male candidates, it may unfairly disadvantage female candidates. Developers must prioritize fairness and inclusivity in their algorithms.

2.2.4 Human-Robot Interaction

The ethical implications of human-robot interaction are multifaceted. As robots become companions, caregivers, or assistants, questions arise regarding their role in society and the nature of their relationships with humans.

2.2.4.1 Example: Care Robots

Care robots designed to assist the elderly or individuals with disabilities can provide significant benefits. However, ethical considerations must address the emotional and psychological impacts of these interactions. Developers should consider the potential for emotional attachment and the implications of relying on robots for companionship.

2.3 Ethical Frameworks for Robotics Development

To address the ethical challenges outlined above, various frameworks have been proposed to guide the development and deployment of robotic systems.

2.3.1 Ethical Guidelines and Principles

Several organizations and institutions have developed ethical guidelines for robotics. These guidelines typically emphasize principles such as:

- **Transparency:** Developers should ensure that the decision-making processes of robots are transparent to users.

- **Accountability:** Clear mechanisms for accountability should be established to address potential harm caused by robotic systems.

- **Inclusivity:** Robotics should promote inclusivity and fairness, considering diverse user needs and perspectives.

- **Privacy Protection:** Developers must implement robust data protection measures to safeguard user privacy.

2.3.2 Stakeholder Engagement

Engaging stakeholders, including users, developers, ethicists, and policymakers, is crucial in developing ethical frameworks. By incorporating diverse perspectives, stakeholders can identify potential ethical dilemmas and work collaboratively to address them.

2.4 Future Directions in Robotics Ethics

As robotics technology continues to evolve, ethical considerations must adapt to address emerging challenges.

2.4.1 Ongoing Research and Development

Research in robotics ethics should be an ongoing effort, focusing on the implications of new technologies and applications. Researchers should explore the ethical dimensions of emerging fields, such as AI-driven robotics and the Internet of Things (IoT).

2.4.2 Legislative and Regulatory Measures

Governments and regulatory bodies play a critical role in shaping the ethical landscape of robotics. Policymakers should work collaboratively with industry experts to develop regulations that address ethical concerns and promote responsible innovation.

2.4.3 Public Awareness and Education

Increasing public awareness of the ethical implications of robotics is essential. Educational initiatives should inform individuals about the potential benefits and risks associated with robotic systems, fostering informed decision-making and promoting responsible use.

Conclusion

Ethical considerations are paramount in the development and deployment of robotic systems. As technology continues to advance, addressing issues of accountability, privacy, bias, and human-robot interaction will be crucial for ensuring responsible innovation. By implementing ethical guidelines, engaging stakeholders, and fostering public awareness, the robotics industry can work towards a future where technology benefits society while minimizing potential harms.

3. Impact of Legislation on Robotics Adoption

The advancement of robotics technology has created significant opportunities across various sectors, including healthcare, manufacturing, and logistics. However, the adoption and integration of robotics are heavily influenced by legislative frameworks and regulations that govern their development, deployment, and use. This section explores the multifaceted impact of legislation on robotics adoption, addressing both the enabling factors that facilitate integration and the potential barriers that may hinder progress. It will provide examples of how different countries and regions have approached robotics legislation, highlighting the need for a balanced regulatory environment that fosters innovation while ensuring safety, security, and ethical considerations. By understanding the interplay between legislation and robotics adoption, stakeholders can better navigate the evolving landscape of this transformative technology.

3.1 The Role of Legislation in Robotics Adoption

Legislation plays a critical role in shaping the environment for robotics adoption. It can either facilitate or impede the growth of robotics by establishing frameworks that govern safety standards, liability, intellectual property, and data protection.

3.1.1 Regulatory Frameworks

Regulatory frameworks set the standards for how robotics technology is developed and used. These regulations can address a wide range of issues, including:

- **Safety Standards:** Ensuring that robotic systems meet safety requirements to protect users and the public.

- **Liability:** Clarifying who is responsible for damages caused by robotic systems.

- **Data Protection:** Safeguarding user privacy and ensuring ethical data usage.

3.1.2 Enabling Innovation

Well-designed legislation can create an environment conducive to innovation. By providing clear guidelines, governments can encourage investment in robotics research and development, fostering a climate of creativity and exploration.

3.2 Case Studies of Legislative Approaches to Robotics

Different countries and regions have adopted various legislative approaches to address the challenges and opportunities posed by robotics.

3.2.1 European Union Regulations

The European Union has been proactive in establishing regulations that govern robotics and artificial intelligence. In April 2021, the European Commission proposed a regulatory framework aimed at ensuring the safe and ethical use of AI and robotics technologies. This framework includes:

- **Risk-based Classification:** Classifying AI systems based on their risk levels, with stricter requirements for higher-risk applications.

- **Transparency and Accountability:** Requiring organizations to disclose information about their AI systems and maintain accountability for their decisions.

Example: The General Data Protection Regulation (GDPR)

The GDPR has significant implications for robotics, particularly in terms of data protection and privacy. Robots that collect, store, or process personal data must comply with GDPR requirements, which can impact how they operate in various settings, such as healthcare or customer service.

3.2.2 United States Regulations

In the United States, the regulatory landscape for robotics is more fragmented, with different states implementing their own rules. However, several federal agencies, including the Occupational Safety and Health Administration (OSHA) and the National Highway Traffic Safety Administration (NHTSA), have begun to address robotics issues.

Example: Autonomous Vehicles

The NHTSA has developed guidelines for the testing and deployment of autonomous vehicles. These guidelines emphasize the importance of safety and provide a framework for manufacturers to demonstrate compliance with safety standards.

3.2.3 Japan's Robotics Strategy

Japan has positioned itself as a global leader in robotics, driven by a national strategy that emphasizes the integration of robotics into various sectors. The Japanese government has introduced several policies to promote robotics, including:

- **Tax Incentives:** Providing tax breaks for companies that invest in robotics technology.

- **Public-Private Partnerships:** Encouraging collaboration between government and industry to foster innovation.

3.3 Barriers to Robotics Adoption Due to Legislation

While legislation can enable robotics adoption, it can also present barriers that hinder progress. These barriers may include:

3.3.1 Complex Regulatory Requirements

In some regions, overly complex or ambiguous regulatory requirements can deter companies from investing in robotics. Uncertainty regarding compliance can lead to hesitancy in adopting new technologies.

3.3.2 Liability Issues

Questions of liability can create a chilling effect on robotics adoption. Companies may be reluctant to deploy autonomous systems if they face uncertainty about their legal responsibilities in the event of accidents or malfunctions.

3.3.3 Slow Legislative Processes

The rapid pace of technological advancement often outstrips the speed of legislative processes. Delays in updating regulations can result in outdated frameworks that do not adequately address emerging technologies.

3.4 Strategies for Navigating Legislation in Robotics

Stakeholders in the robotics sector can adopt several strategies to navigate the legislative landscape effectively.

3.4.1 Collaboration with Policymakers

Engaging with policymakers and regulatory bodies can help ensure that legislation aligns with industry needs.

Collaborative efforts can lead to more informed decision-making and responsive regulatory frameworks.

3.4.2 Advocacy for Clear Standards

Industry stakeholders can advocate for the establishment of clear and consistent standards that promote innovation while ensuring safety and ethical considerations. By working together, companies can influence legislative outcomes that support robotics adoption.

3.4.3 Education and Awareness

Raising awareness about the benefits of robotics and the importance of balanced regulations can help shift public perception and influence legislative priorities. Educational initiatives can inform stakeholders about the potential of robotics to drive economic growth and improve quality of life.

Conclusion

Legislation plays a pivotal role in shaping the landscape for robotics adoption. By establishing regulatory frameworks that promote safety, accountability, and innovation, governments can foster an environment conducive to the growth of robotics technology. However, stakeholders must also be aware of the barriers that legislation can pose and work collaboratively to navigate these challenges. As robotics continues to evolve, a proactive approach to legislation will be essential to harnessing the full potential of this transformative technology.

4. Privacy Concerns and Data Security in Robotics

As robotics technology continues to advance and permeate various sectors, concerns related to privacy and data security have emerged as significant challenges. Robotic systems often collect, process, and store vast amounts of data, including personal and sensitive information, raising questions about how this data is used, who has access to it, and the measures in place to protect it. This section explores the critical privacy and data security issues associated with robotics, highlighting the implications for individuals and organizations. By examining case studies and real-world examples, we can better understand the complexities of ensuring data security in robotics and the necessary frameworks to mitigate risks. As we delve into these challenges, we will also discuss the potential solutions and best practices for safeguarding privacy in the age of robotics.

4.1 Understanding Privacy and Data Security in Robotics

Robotic systems operate across various industries, including healthcare, manufacturing, and personal assistance, all of which require the collection and processing of data. Understanding privacy and data security in this context involves exploring the types of data collected, the technologies used, and the potential risks involved.

4.1.1 Types of Data Collected by Robots

Robots can collect various types of data, including:

- **Personal Data:** Information that can identify an individual, such as names, addresses, and contact details.

- **Behavioral Data:** Data related to user interactions, preferences, and habits.

- **Sensor Data:** Information collected from the robot's sensors, which may include audio, video, and environmental data.

4.1.2 Technologies Used in Robotics

Robotics technologies encompass a wide range of systems and applications. Key technologies include:

- **Artificial Intelligence (AI):** AI algorithms enable robots to process data, make decisions, and learn from interactions.

- **Internet of Things (IoT):** IoT devices connect robots to the internet, allowing data collection and communication with other devices.

- **Cloud Computing:** Cloud platforms provide storage and processing capabilities for the vast amounts of data generated by robotic systems.

4.1.3 Potential Risks to Privacy and Data Security

The use of robotics raises several privacy and data security concerns, including:

- **Unauthorized Access:** Data breaches can occur if unauthorized individuals gain access to sensitive information.

- **Data Misuse:** Collected data may be used for unintended purposes, such as profiling or surveillance.

- **Insufficient Security Measures:** Weak security protocols can expose robotic systems to cyberattacks, putting data at risk.

4.2 Case Studies Highlighting Privacy Concerns in Robotics

Examining real-world examples can provide insight into the privacy challenges faced by robotic systems.

4.2.1 Healthcare Robotics

In the healthcare sector, surgical robots and robotic-assisted therapies often collect sensitive patient data. For instance, the da Vinci Surgical System, used for minimally invasive surgeries, collects data on patient anatomy and surgical performance.

Example: Data Breaches in Healthcare

A notable example occurred in 2018 when a breach of the health information system of a prominent hospital revealed sensitive patient data due to vulnerabilities in the robotic systems used. This incident raised concerns about how patient data is protected during robotic procedures and the need for robust security measures.

4.2.2 Surveillance Robots

Robots equipped with cameras and sensors for surveillance purposes have raised significant privacy concerns. These robots are used in various settings, from public spaces to private properties.

Example: Security Drones

Security drones deployed in urban areas for monitoring can collect extensive video data of individuals without their consent. This has sparked debates about the ethics of surveillance and the need for regulations to protect citizens' privacy rights.

4.3 Data Security Challenges in Robotics

Data security in robotics involves addressing several key challenges:

4.3.1 Cybersecurity Threats

Robotic systems are increasingly targeted by cyberattacks due to their connectivity and reliance on data. Cyber threats can lead to unauthorized access, data breaches, and even manipulation of robotic functions.

Example: Cyberattacks on Industrial Robots

In 2020, an attack on a manufacturing facility's robotic systems disrupted operations and resulted in the loss of sensitive production data. This incident underscores the importance of implementing strong cybersecurity measures to protect robotic systems from malicious attacks.

4.3.2 Compliance with Data Protection Regulations

Robotics companies must navigate various data protection regulations, such as the General Data Protection Regulation (GDPR) in Europe, which imposes strict requirements on how personal data is collected, processed, and stored.

4.3.3 Data Ownership and Consent

Determining data ownership and obtaining consent for data collection can be complex in robotics. Users may not fully understand how their data is collected and used, leading to potential violations of privacy rights.

4.4 Solutions for Enhancing Privacy and Data Security in Robotics

To address privacy and data security concerns in robotics, several solutions can be implemented:

4.4.1 Robust Security Protocols

Developing and implementing strong security protocols is essential for protecting robotic systems from cyber threats. This includes encryption, authentication, and regular security assessments.

4.4.2 Privacy by Design

Integrating privacy considerations into the design phase of robotic systems can help ensure that data protection measures are built-in from the outset. This approach can involve:

- **Data Minimization:** Collecting only the data necessary for a specific purpose.

- **Anonymization:** Removing identifiable information to protect user privacy.

4.4.3 User Education and Awareness

Educating users about the data collection practices of robotic systems and the importance of privacy can empower individuals to make informed decisions. Transparency about data usage can also foster trust in robotic technologies.

4.5 Future Directions for Privacy and Data Security in Robotics

As robotics technology continues to evolve, addressing privacy and data security will remain a top priority. Future directions may include:

4.5.1 Development of International Standards

Establishing international standards for data protection in robotics can provide a unified approach to addressing privacy concerns and ensuring consistent practices across borders.

4.5.2 Collaboration between Industry and Regulators

Collaboration between the robotics industry and regulatory bodies can help develop effective policies that balance innovation with privacy protections.

4.5.3 Advancements in Secure Robotics Technologies

Investing in research and development of secure robotics technologies will be crucial for enhancing privacy and data security. This may involve exploring new encryption methods, secure communication protocols, and AI-driven security solutions.

Conclusion

Privacy concerns and data security are critical challenges that must be addressed as robotics technology continues to advance. By understanding the types of data collected, the risks involved, and the potential solutions, stakeholders can work together to create a secure and privacy-respecting environment for robotics adoption. The future of robotics hinges on the ability to safeguard user privacy while harnessing the transformative potential of this technology.

5. Future Directions for Robotics Regulation and Ethics

As robotics technology rapidly evolves and becomes increasingly integrated into various sectors, the need for comprehensive regulatory and ethical frameworks is more pressing than ever. The potential benefits of robotics—ranging from increased efficiency and productivity to enhanced quality of life—must be balanced with the associated risks and ethical dilemmas. This section explores future directions for robotics regulation and ethics, considering the implications of emerging technologies and societal expectations. We will examine the challenges faced by regulators, the role of stakeholders, and the need for adaptive regulatory frameworks that can keep pace with technological advancements. By analyzing real-world examples and proposing forward-thinking solutions, we aim to contribute to the ongoing discourse on how to responsibly harness the power of robotics while safeguarding public interests.

5.1 The Current Landscape of Robotics Regulation and Ethics

To understand the future directions for robotics regulation and ethics, it is essential to assess the current landscape. Robotics regulation encompasses a range of legal, ethical, and safety considerations that govern the design, development, and deployment of robotic systems.

5.1.1 Regulatory Challenges

Robotics regulation faces several challenges, including:

- **Rapid Technological Advancements:** The pace at which robotics technology is evolving often outstrips the ability of regulators to develop appropriate frameworks.

- **Diverse Applications:** Robotics is applied across various sectors, from healthcare to manufacturing, requiring tailored regulations that address sector-specific concerns.

- **Global Variability:** Regulatory approaches differ significantly between countries, leading to inconsistencies in standards and practices.

5.1.2 Ethical Considerations

Ethical considerations in robotics encompass a wide array of issues, such as:

- **Autonomy and Decision-Making:** The ethical implications of granting robots autonomy in decision-making processes, especially in sensitive areas like healthcare and law enforcement.

- **Accountability:** Determining who is responsible for the actions of robots, particularly in the event of errors or accidents.

- **Bias and Fairness:** Addressing issues of algorithmic bias and ensuring that robotic systems operate fairly and equitably.

5.2 The Role of Stakeholders in Robotics Regulation

A collaborative approach involving various stakeholders is essential for effective robotics regulation. Key stakeholders include:

5.2.1 Governments and Regulatory Bodies

Governments play a crucial role in establishing regulatory frameworks that protect public interests while promoting innovation. Effective governance requires:

- **Multi-Stakeholder Engagement:** Involving industry experts, academia, and civil society in the regulatory process to ensure diverse perspectives are considered.

- **Adaptive Regulations:** Developing regulations that can evolve with technological advancements and societal changes.

5.2.2 Industry and Manufacturers

Robotics manufacturers have a responsibility to prioritize ethical considerations in their design and development processes. This includes:

- **Implementing Best Practices:** Adopting industry standards and best practices for safety, data protection, and ethical AI use.

- **Transparency:** Providing clear information about how robotic systems operate and the data they collect.

5.2.3 Civil Society and Advocacy Groups

Civil society organizations play a vital role in advocating for ethical practices and holding stakeholders accountable. Their contributions include:

- **Raising Awareness:** Educating the public about the implications of robotics and advocating for responsible practices.

- **Policy Advocacy:** Engaging with policymakers to influence the development of regulations that prioritize ethical considerations.

5.3 Emerging Trends Influencing Robotics Regulation

Several emerging trends are shaping the future of robotics regulation and ethics:

5.3.1 The Rise of Artificial Intelligence

As AI becomes increasingly integrated into robotic systems, the regulatory landscape must adapt to address unique challenges. This includes:

- **Algorithmic Accountability:** Ensuring that AI algorithms used in robotics are transparent, interpretable, and free from bias.

- **Ethical AI Frameworks:** Developing guidelines and standards for the ethical use of AI in robotics.

5.3.2 The Internet of Things (IoT)

The interconnectedness of robotic systems through IoT raises additional regulatory concerns related to data security and privacy. Key considerations include:

- **Data Ownership and Consent:** Clarifying who owns the data generated by robotic systems and how consent is obtained for data collection.

- **Cybersecurity Regulations:** Implementing robust cybersecurity measures to protect connected robotic systems from cyber threats.

5.3.3 Global Cooperation

As robotics technology transcends national borders, international cooperation is essential for establishing consistent regulatory frameworks. This can involve:

- **Harmonizing Standards:** Working towards globally accepted standards for robotics safety and ethics.

- **Collaborative Research Initiatives:** Engaging in joint research efforts to address common challenges in robotics regulation.

5.4 Proposing Future Regulatory Frameworks

Developing effective regulatory frameworks for robotics requires innovative approaches that address the unique characteristics of robotic systems.

5.4.1 Flexible and Adaptive Regulations

Regulatory frameworks should be flexible and adaptive, allowing for adjustments as technology evolves. This can be achieved through:

- **Sandbox Approaches:** Creating regulatory sandboxes that allow companies to test new technologies in a controlled environment without facing stringent regulatory hurdles.

- **Periodic Reviews:** Establishing mechanisms for periodic reviews of regulations to ensure they remain relevant and effective.

5.4.2 Ethical Guidelines and Standards

The establishment of ethical guidelines and standards for robotics can help ensure responsible development and deployment. This may involve:

- **Developing Ethical Codes:** Collaborating with industry stakeholders to create ethical codes of conduct for robotics development.

- **Promoting Certification Programs:** Encouraging certification programs that verify compliance with ethical standards.

5.4.3 Public Engagement and Education

Engaging the public in discussions about robotics regulation can foster transparency and trust. Strategies for public engagement include:

- **Public Consultations:** Conducting public consultations to gather input on regulatory proposals and ethical considerations.

- **Educational Initiatives:** Implementing educational initiatives that inform the public about the benefits and risks of robotics technology.

5.5 Conclusion

The future of robotics regulation and ethics hinges on the ability to balance innovation with public safety and ethical considerations. By fostering collaboration among stakeholders, embracing emerging trends, and proposing adaptive regulatory frameworks, we can navigate the complexities of robotics technology responsibly. As we move forward, it is essential to prioritize ethical principles and ensure that the benefits of robotics are harnessed in a manner that respects individual rights and promotes societal well-being.

Chapter 9: Challenges and Opportunities

1. Technical Challenges Facing the Robotics Industry
2. Economic and Market Opportunities
3. Addressing Public Concerns about Job Displacement
4. Infrastructure Challenges for Widespread Robotics Adoption
5. Opportunities in Emerging Markets and Developing Countries

Chapter 9

Challenges and Opportunities

Introduction

The robotics industry stands at a pivotal crossroads, characterized by both significant challenges and remarkable opportunities. As robotics technologies continue to evolve and permeate various sectors—from manufacturing and healthcare to logistics and agriculture—their impact on society becomes increasingly profound. However, this transformative potential is not without obstacles. Technical challenges, economic considerations, and public apprehensions regarding job displacement pose significant hurdles to widespread adoption.

This chapter delves into the multifaceted landscape of the robotics industry, exploring the technical challenges that innovators face in developing and deploying effective robotic solutions. We will also examine the economic opportunities that arise from advancing robotics technologies, including new market prospects and the potential for enhanced productivity. Additionally, we will address public concerns about job displacement, emphasizing the importance of proactive measures to mitigate these effects and foster workforce adaptability.

Furthermore, this chapter will highlight infrastructure challenges that must be overcome to facilitate the seamless integration of robotics into existing systems. Finally, we will explore the untapped potential of emerging markets and developing countries, where robotics could play a vital role in driving economic growth and improving quality of life. By analyzing these challenges and opportunities, this chapter aims to provide a comprehensive understanding of the current state and future trajectory of the robotics industry, paving the way for informed discussions and strategic decision-making.

1. Technical Challenges Facing the Robotics Industry

The robotics industry is experiencing rapid advancements, driven by technological innovations and the increasing demand for automation across various sectors. From manufacturing and healthcare to logistics and agriculture, robots are being integrated into processes to enhance efficiency, reduce human labor, and improve precision. However, despite these advancements, the industry faces several technical challenges that impede the widespread adoption and optimal performance of robotic systems.

These challenges can be categorized into five main areas: perception, mobility, manipulation, human-robot interaction, and autonomy. Each of these areas presents unique hurdles that engineers and researchers must overcome to enhance the capabilities and reliability of robotic systems. This chapter will delve into these technical challenges in detail, illustrating each issue with relevant examples and potential solutions.

1.1 Perception Challenges

Perception is crucial for robots to interact effectively with their environment. Robots rely on sensors to gather data about their surroundings, which they then process to make informed decisions. However, the complexity of real-world environments presents significant challenges.

1.1.1 Sensor Limitations

Most robotic systems use a variety of sensors, such as cameras, LiDAR, and ultrasonic sensors, to gather environmental data. However, these sensors have limitations. For instance, cameras may struggle with varying lighting conditions, and LiDAR can be affected by rain or fog. As a result, robots may not always accurately perceive their surroundings, leading to errors in navigation or interaction.

1.1.2 Object Recognition

Another significant challenge in perception is object recognition. Robots must accurately identify and classify objects to interact with them appropriately. Machine learning algorithms have improved object recognition capabilities, but they still face difficulties in recognizing objects in cluttered or dynamic environments. For example, a robotic arm designed for warehouse operations may misidentify items on a shelf due to overlapping or poorly illuminated objects.

1.2 Mobility Challenges

Mobility refers to a robot's ability to navigate its environment effectively. Different types of robots face distinct mobility challenges based on their design and application.

1.2.1 Terrain Navigation

Robots designed for outdoor environments, such as agricultural robots or drones, must navigate various terrains, including uneven ground, slopes, and obstacles. For instance, an agricultural robot may need to traverse fields with different soil conditions, which can affect its movement and stability. Engineers must develop robust algorithms that enable robots to adapt to changing terrains while maintaining balance and speed.

1.2.2 Dynamic Environments

In contrast, robots operating in dynamic environments, such as warehouses or factories, must navigate around moving objects, including human workers and other machines. This requires advanced algorithms that can predict the movement of these entities and adjust the robot's path accordingly. For example, autonomous mobile robots used in warehouses must constantly update their navigation plans to avoid collisions with humans and other robots.

1.3 Manipulation Challenges

Manipulation refers to a robot's ability to grasp, move, and interact with objects. This area presents numerous technical challenges, particularly regarding dexterity and precision.

1.3.1 Grasping and Handling

Robots must be able to grasp and manipulate objects of varying shapes, sizes, and weights. Traditional robotic grippers often struggle with irregularly shaped or delicate items. For instance, a robotic arm designed for assembly tasks may find it challenging to pick up a fragile glass component without breaking it. Researchers are exploring soft robotics and adaptive grippers to enhance manipulation capabilities.

1.3.2 Task Generalization

Another challenge is enabling robots to generalize their manipulation skills across different tasks. A robot trained to assemble one type of product may not be able to adapt its skills to assemble a different product without significant retraining. This lack of versatility limits the practicality of robots in dynamic production environments where product lines frequently change.

1.4 Human-Robot Interaction Challenges

Human-robot interaction is essential for robots working alongside humans in collaborative settings. Ensuring safe and efficient interaction is a significant challenge.

1.4.1 Communication and Understanding

Effective communication between humans and robots is crucial for collaboration. Robots must be able to interpret human commands, gestures, and intentions accurately. For example, if a human worker signals for assistance, the robot must understand the context and respond appropriately. Natural language processing and gesture recognition technologies are critical in addressing these challenges.

1.4.2 Safety Concerns

Safety is a paramount concern in human-robot interaction. Robots must be designed to operate safely alongside humans, minimizing the risk of accidents. For example, collaborative robots (cobots) must have built-in safety features that prevent them from causing harm to human workers during operation. Engineers must develop reliable safety systems that allow robots to function effectively without compromising worker safety.

1.5 Autonomy Challenges

Autonomy refers to a robot's ability to operate independently without human intervention. While advancements have been made, achieving full autonomy remains a challenge.

1.5.1 Decision-Making and Control

Robots must be equipped with sophisticated algorithms that enable them to make decisions based on environmental data. For example, an autonomous delivery robot must decide the best route to navigate obstacles and reach its destination efficiently. Developing algorithms that can process vast amounts of data in real-time is a significant challenge.

1.5.2 Reliability and Robustness

The reliability of autonomous systems is critical, especially in applications such as autonomous vehicles or surgical robots. Engineers must ensure that robots can consistently perform their tasks without failure. For instance, a self-driving car must accurately perceive its surroundings and respond to unexpected situations, such as sudden obstacles or changing traffic conditions. Achieving high reliability requires extensive testing and validation of algorithms.

Conclusion

The technical challenges facing the robotics industry are multifaceted and complex. Addressing these challenges requires ongoing research and innovation in various areas, including perception, mobility, manipulation, human-robot interaction, and autonomy. By overcoming these hurdles, the robotics industry can continue to advance, leading to more capable and effective robotic systems that can positively impact numerous sectors.

2. Economic and Market Opportunities

The robotics industry is at the forefront of technological advancement, creating new economic opportunities across various sectors. As automation becomes increasingly integrated into daily operations, businesses are recognizing the potential of robotics to enhance productivity, reduce operational costs, and drive innovation. This chapter will explore the economic and market opportunities presented by robotics, focusing on various industries, the impact of robotics on job creation and displacement, and emerging trends that shape the future of the market.

The global robotics market is expected to grow significantly, driven by advancements in artificial intelligence (AI), machine learning, and sensor technologies. According to a report by Grand View Research, the global robotics market was valued at approximately $39.8 billion in 2020 and is projected to reach $100.5 billion by 2025, growing at a compound annual growth rate (CAGR) of 20.5% . This growth presents numerous opportunities for businesses, investors, and entrepreneurs to capitalize on emerging technologies and changing consumer demands.

2.1 Industry-Specific Opportunities

2.1.1 Manufacturing

Manufacturing is one of the earliest adopters of robotics, and it continues to offer significant opportunities for growth. Robotics technologies enhance efficiency, accuracy, and safety in production processes. For instance, collaborative robots (cobots) are designed to work alongside human operators, enabling a seamless integration of human and machine capabilities. Companies like Universal Robots have successfully implemented cobots in various manufacturing applications, reducing production time and increasing output.

Additionally, the rise of Industry 4.0 has further accelerated the adoption of robotics in manufacturing. Smart factories leverage IoT and robotics to create interconnected systems that optimize production and supply chain management. This integration results in improved resource utilization and reduced waste, ultimately contributing to a more sustainable manufacturing environment.

2.1.2 Healthcare

The healthcare sector is increasingly utilizing robotics to improve patient care and operational efficiency. Surgical robots, such as the da Vinci Surgical System, enable surgeons to perform minimally invasive procedures with enhanced precision, leading to shorter recovery times and reduced complications . Moreover, robotic-assisted rehabilitation devices are being used to aid patients in their recovery, offering personalized therapy and monitoring progress.

Telepresence robots are also gaining traction in healthcare settings, allowing remote consultations and support for patients and healthcare providers. The COVID-19 pandemic has accelerated the adoption of these technologies, highlighting their potential to enhance healthcare delivery and access.

2.1.3 Logistics and Warehousing

The logistics and warehousing sectors are undergoing significant transformations due to the integration of robotics. Automated guided vehicles (AGVs) and autonomous mobile robots (AMRs) are increasingly used to streamline material handling, inventory management, and order fulfillment processes. Companies like Amazon and Walmart are leveraging robotics to enhance efficiency in their supply chains, enabling faster delivery times and reduced operational costs .

As e-commerce continues to grow, the demand for robotic solutions in logistics will likely increase. Innovations in drone delivery and last-mile logistics are expected to create new market opportunities, allowing businesses to meet consumer expectations for rapid and reliable delivery.

2.1.4 Agriculture

Agriculture is another sector poised for significant growth through robotics adoption. Agricultural robots, such as drones for crop monitoring and autonomous tractors for planting and harvesting, are revolutionizing traditional farming practices. These technologies enable farmers to optimize resource utilization, increase yields, and reduce labor costs.

For example, companies like PrecisionHawk are utilizing drones equipped with advanced sensors to monitor crop health and assess field conditions. This data-driven approach allows farmers to make informed decisions about irrigation, fertilization, and pest control, ultimately improving productivity and sustainability in agriculture.

2.2 Economic Impact of Robotics

2.2.1 Job Creation vs. Job Displacement

One of the most debated aspects of robotics adoption is its impact on employment. While automation can lead to job displacement in certain sectors, it also creates new job opportunities in others. For instance, the demand for skilled workers to design, program, and maintain robotic systems is increasing as automation becomes more prevalent.

According to a report by the World Economic Forum, automation could create 97 million new jobs by 2025 while displacing 85 million jobs . This shift highlights the need for workforce reskilling and upskilling programs to prepare employees for the changing job landscape.

2.2.2 Increased Productivity and Economic Growth

Robotics also contributes to increased productivity and economic growth. By automating repetitive tasks, businesses can allocate human resources to higher-value activities, fostering innovation and creativity. This shift not only enhances operational efficiency but also drives economic growth through increased output and competitiveness.

For example, a study conducted by McKinsey Global Institute estimated that by 2030, automation could increase global labor productivity by up to 1.4% annually . This increase in productivity can lead to higher GDP growth rates, benefitting economies worldwide.

2.3 Emerging Market Opportunities

2.3.1 Startups and Innovation

The robotics market is witnessing a surge in startups and innovative companies that are developing cutting-edge technologies. These startups are exploring new applications for robotics, from household robots to advanced industrial automation solutions. Venture capital investment in robotics has increased significantly, with investors recognizing the potential for high returns in this rapidly evolving market.

For instance, companies like Boston Dynamics and OpenAI are pushing the boundaries of robotics and AI, attracting significant investments and attention from industries worldwide. This wave of innovation is likely to lead to the emergence of new market segments and business models.

2.3.2 Global Expansion

As robotics technologies continue to mature, opportunities for global expansion are increasing. Emerging markets, particularly in Asia and Africa, present significant potential for robotics adoption. Rapid urbanization, population growth, and increasing labor costs in these regions create a favorable environment for robotic solutions across various sectors, including manufacturing, healthcare, and agriculture.

For example, China has positioned itself as a leader in robotics adoption, with government initiatives aimed at boosting domestic production and innovation in the robotics sector. This trend is likely to continue, presenting opportunities for foreign companies to collaborate with local firms and expand their presence in these markets.

Conclusion

The economic and market opportunities presented by robotics are vast and varied, encompassing numerous industries and applications. As technological advancements continue to reshape the landscape, businesses and entrepreneurs must remain adaptable and forward-thinking to capitalize on these opportunities. By embracing robotics, organizations can enhance productivity, drive innovation, and contribute to sustainable economic growth.

3. Addressing Public Concerns about Job Displacement

The rise of robotics and automation technologies has sparked significant public concern regarding job displacement. As machines and algorithms increasingly take over tasks traditionally performed by humans, many workers fear losing their jobs or facing reduced opportunities for employment. This chapter addresses these concerns by exploring the nature of job displacement caused by robotics, examining historical precedents, analyzing potential solutions, and highlighting the new job opportunities created by automation. By providing a comprehensive overview of this critical issue, we can foster a more informed public discourse about the future of work in an increasingly automated world.

Job displacement is not a new phenomenon; throughout history, technological advancements have led to changes in the labor market. For example, the Industrial Revolution saw many skilled artisans and craftspeople lose their livelihoods as factories and mechanized production became more prevalent. However, this disruption also led to the creation of new jobs in manufacturing, transportation, and logistics. Similarly, while robotics and automation may displace certain jobs today, they also hold the potential to create new opportunities and industries, ultimately transforming the nature of work.

The World Economic Forum estimates that by 2025, automation could displace 85 million jobs globally, but it could also create 97 million new roles as the demand for skilled labor in areas such as technology, engineering, and healthcare continues to grow. Addressing public concerns about job displacement is essential for fostering acceptance of automation technologies and ensuring a smooth transition for affected workers.

3.1 Understanding Job Displacement

3.1.1 The Nature of Job Displacement

Job displacement occurs when workers lose their jobs due to factors such as automation, outsourcing, or economic shifts. In the context of robotics, automation can lead to the elimination of specific tasks within jobs, making certain positions redundant. For instance, assembly line jobs in manufacturing have increasingly been replaced by robotic systems that can perform repetitive tasks more efficiently and accurately.

It's essential to differentiate between job displacement and job loss. Job displacement refers to the involuntary transition of workers from one job to another or from one sector to another, while job loss signifies the complete loss of employment. Automation often leads to the former, as workers may be retrained or transition to new roles rather than being entirely removed from the labor force.

3.1.2 Historical Perspectives

Throughout history, technological advancements have resulted in job displacement, but they have also led to the emergence of new opportunities. For instance, during the agricultural revolution, the introduction of mechanized farming equipment displaced many laborers but also paved the way for the development of the food processing and distribution industries.

Similarly, in the late 20th century, the rise of computers and information technology transformed various sectors, leading to job losses in certain areas while creating opportunities in others, such as IT support, software development, and data analysis. Learning from these historical precedents can help us better understand the potential impact of robotics on employment and the importance of adaptation and reskilling.

3.2 The Impact of Robotics on Employment

3.2.1 Job Displacement Across Sectors

The impact of robotics on employment varies across industries. Manufacturing, logistics, and retail are among the sectors most affected by automation. In manufacturing, robots are increasingly used for tasks such as welding, painting, and assembly. According to the International Federation of Robotics (IFR), the adoption of industrial robots increased by 12% globally in 2020, leading to concerns about job displacement among factory workers.

In logistics, the rise of automated systems for inventory management, order fulfillment, and delivery has the potential to displace a significant number of jobs. For example, Amazon has been a leader in automating its warehouses with robotic systems, leading to increased efficiency but also concerns about job security for warehouse workers.

In retail, the growing trend of self-checkout systems and automated customer service has raised alarms about job displacement among cashiers and sales associates. As technology continues to advance, it's crucial to assess the extent of job displacement and identify strategies to address the concerns of affected workers.

3.2.2 New Job Opportunities

Despite concerns about job displacement, robotics and automation also create new job opportunities. For example, the demand for skilled workers in robotics design, programming, and maintenance is increasing. As businesses adopt automation technologies, they require employees with specialized skills to develop and manage these systems.

Furthermore, new industries and sectors are emerging as a result of technological advancements. For instance, the growth of the electric vehicle industry has created jobs in manufacturing, research, and infrastructure development. Similarly, the expansion of renewable energy technologies has led to job creation in areas such as solar panel installation and wind turbine maintenance.

3.3 Strategies for Addressing Job Displacement Concerns

3.3.1 Reskilling and Upskilling

One of the most effective strategies for addressing job displacement concerns is reskilling and upskilling the workforce. Governments, businesses, and educational institutions must collaborate to provide training programs that equip workers with the skills needed for emerging job opportunities. For instance, initiatives such as apprenticeships, vocational training, and online courses can help workers transition to new roles in technology, healthcare, and other high-demand sectors.

Companies like Amazon have invested in employee training programs to help workers transition to new roles within the organization, including opportunities in technology and management. These programs not only help mitigate the impact of job displacement but also foster a culture of continuous learning and adaptability.

3.3.2 Policy Interventions

Governments play a crucial role in addressing job displacement concerns through policy interventions. Implementing policies that promote workforce development, provide safety nets for displaced workers, and support job creation in emerging industries can help alleviate public fears about automation.

For example, the introduction of universal basic income (UBI) has been proposed as a potential solution to provide financial support to individuals facing job displacement. While UBI remains a topic of debate, it highlights the importance of exploring innovative approaches to support workers in a rapidly changing labor market.

3.4 Public Awareness and Communication

3.4.1 Fostering Public Discourse

Creating an informed public discourse around robotics and job displacement is essential for alleviating concerns. Companies, policymakers, and educators should engage with communities to raise awareness about the benefits and potential challenges of automation. Open communication about the changing job landscape can help build public trust and acceptance of new technologies.

3.4.2 Case Studies and Success Stories

Highlighting case studies and success stories of companies and individuals who have successfully transitioned to new roles can inspire confidence in the workforce. For example, showcasing workers who have reskilled and found success in technology or other emerging sectors can help dispel fears and demonstrate the potential for growth and opportunity in an automated world.

Conclusion

Addressing public concerns about job displacement due to robotics and automation is critical for ensuring a smooth transition into an increasingly automated future. By understanding the nature of job displacement, examining historical precedents, and implementing strategies for reskilling and policy interventions, we can foster a more resilient workforce that is equipped to thrive in a changing labor market. While challenges exist, the potential for new job opportunities and economic growth can help mitigate the impact of job displacement, ultimately benefiting society as a whole.

4. Infrastructure Challenges for Widespread Robotics Adoption

The adoption of robotics across various sectors is increasingly seen as a pivotal element in driving efficiency, innovation, and productivity. However, the widespread integration of robotics faces significant infrastructure challenges that must be addressed to fully realize the potential of these technologies. This chapter explores the multifaceted infrastructure challenges hindering the adoption of robotics, including technological, physical, and regulatory barriers. By examining these challenges, we can identify potential solutions and highlight the importance of strategic investments in infrastructure to facilitate a smoother transition to an automated future.

The growing trend toward automation is evident in industries such as manufacturing, logistics, healthcare, and agriculture. However, many organizations encounter obstacles that prevent them from fully leveraging robotic technologies. A report by McKinsey Global Institute highlights that, despite the potential for automation to transform economies, only 50% of organizations have successfully integrated robotic systems into their operations. This chapter will delve into the underlying infrastructure issues contributing to this lag, drawing on real-world examples and case studies to illustrate the challenges and potential solutions.

4.1 Understanding Infrastructure Challenges

4.1.1 Definition of Infrastructure in Robotics Context

Infrastructure, in the context of robotics adoption, refers to the foundational systems, services, and structures that support the deployment and operation of robotic technologies. This encompasses a wide range of elements, including physical facilities, technological networks, regulatory frameworks, and skilled workforce development. Each component plays a critical role in enabling organizations to adopt and integrate robotics into their processes effectively.

4.1.2 Importance of Robust Infrastructure

A robust infrastructure is essential for the successful implementation of robotics. It provides the necessary foundation for seamless communication, data exchange, and operational efficiency. Without adequate infrastructure, organizations may struggle to optimize their robotic systems, resulting in lower productivity and potential financial losses. For instance, the inability to effectively integrate robotics with existing IT systems can lead to data silos, miscommunication, and inefficient operations.

4.2 Technological Infrastructure Challenges

4.2.1 Compatibility and Interoperability

One of the primary technological challenges in robotics adoption is ensuring compatibility and interoperability among different systems and devices. As organizations integrate various robotic technologies, they often encounter issues related to the integration of legacy systems with newer technologies. For example, manufacturing companies may have existing machinery that is not compatible with modern robotic systems, leading to inefficiencies and increased costs.

4.2.2 Network Connectivity and Data Management

The effective operation of robotics relies heavily on network connectivity and data management. Organizations must ensure that they have robust communication networks in place to facilitate real-time data exchange between robotic systems and other components of the operational ecosystem. For instance, in warehouse automation, a lack of high-speed internet connectivity can hinder the performance of autonomous vehicles and robotic picking systems, ultimately affecting order fulfillment and inventory management.

4.2.3 Cybersecurity Concerns

As robotic systems become more interconnected, cybersecurity concerns also emerge. The integration of robotics into critical infrastructure raises the stakes for data breaches and cyber-attacks. For example, a cyberattack on an automated manufacturing facility could disrupt production lines and compromise sensitive data. Organizations must prioritize cybersecurity measures to protect their robotic systems and ensure operational continuity.

4.3 Physical Infrastructure Challenges

4.3.1 Facility Design and Layout

The physical layout of facilities can significantly impact the adoption of robotics. For instance, traditional warehouse designs may not be conducive to the integration of autonomous robots. Companies must evaluate and redesign their facilities to optimize the flow of materials and the movement of robotic systems. A case study of a leading logistics company revealed that by reconfiguring its warehouse layout to accommodate autonomous vehicles, it was able to improve efficiency and reduce operational costs.

4.3.2 Maintenance and Upkeep

Maintaining robotic systems and the physical infrastructure supporting them is crucial for sustained operations. Organizations must develop maintenance protocols and invest in preventive measures to ensure that both robotic systems and supporting infrastructure remain in optimal condition. Neglecting maintenance can lead to costly downtimes and decreased productivity. For example, a manufacturing facility that failed to implement a regular maintenance schedule for its robotic arms experienced frequent breakdowns, resulting in lost production time and revenue.

4.3.3 Accessibility and Scalability

Accessibility to robotic technologies can also be a challenge, particularly for small and medium-sized enterprises (SMEs) that may lack the necessary resources to invest in advanced infrastructure. To promote widespread robotics adoption, it is essential to create scalable solutions that can be tailored to the specific needs of different organizations. For instance, cloud-based robotic systems can offer SMEs access to advanced capabilities without requiring significant upfront investments in infrastructure.

4.4 Regulatory and Policy Challenges

4.4.1 Lack of Standardization

The absence of standardized regulations and guidelines for robotic technologies can create uncertainty for organizations considering adoption. Without clear standards, companies may face challenges in ensuring compliance with safety regulations and industry best practices. For example, the lack of standardized protocols for collaborative robots (cobots) operating alongside human workers can lead to safety concerns and hinder their integration into existing workflows.

4.4.2 Government Incentives and Support

Government policies play a critical role in shaping the adoption of robotics. Effective policies can promote investment in infrastructure, provide funding for research and development, and support workforce training initiatives. However, inadequate government support can deter organizations from investing in robotic technologies. Countries like Germany and South Korea have implemented robust government programs to incentivize robotics adoption, leading to increased investment and growth in the sector.

4.4.3 Public Perception and Acceptance

Public perception of robotics also influences adoption rates. Concerns about job displacement, safety, and ethical implications can create resistance to the widespread use of robotic technologies. Organizations must engage with stakeholders, including employees, customers, and communities, to address concerns and foster acceptance of robotics. Transparent communication about the benefits and safety measures associated with robotics can help alleviate public apprehensions.

4.5 Strategies for Overcoming Infrastructure Challenges

4.5.1 Collaborative Efforts

Addressing infrastructure challenges requires collaboration among various stakeholders, including businesses, government agencies, educational institutions, and industry associations. Collaborative efforts can facilitate knowledge sharing, resource allocation, and the development of standardized practices. For example, industry consortiums can work together to establish best practices for integrating robotics into existing infrastructure.

4.5.2 Investment in Research and Development

Investing in research and development is essential for advancing robotics technologies and addressing infrastructure challenges. Organizations should allocate resources toward developing innovative solutions that enhance interoperability, improve cybersecurity, and optimize facility layouts for robotic systems. Public-private partnerships can also drive R&D efforts and accelerate technological advancements.

4.5.3 Workforce Development Programs

To support the adoption of robotics, organizations must invest in workforce development programs that equip employees with the necessary skills to operate and maintain robotic systems. Training initiatives can help bridge the skills gap and ensure a smooth transition to an automated workforce. For instance, partnerships with technical colleges and universities can provide training programs focused on robotics and automation technologies.

Conclusion

The widespread adoption of robotics presents both challenges and opportunities for organizations across various sectors. Addressing infrastructure challenges—ranging from technological and physical barriers to regulatory and policy issues—is crucial for unlocking the full potential of robotics. By investing in robust infrastructure, fostering collaboration among stakeholders, and prioritizing workforce development, organizations can pave the way for successful robotics integration. As we continue to navigate the complexities of an automated future, strategic investments in infrastructure will be key to driving innovation and enhancing productivity in a rapidly evolving global landscape.

5. Opportunities in Emerging Markets and Developing Countries

The global landscape of robotics is rapidly evolving, presenting a myriad of opportunities, particularly in emerging markets and developing countries. As these regions strive for economic growth, technological advancement, and improved living standards, robotics offers a transformative solution across various sectors. This chapter will explore the numerous opportunities available in these markets, highlighting the potential benefits of robotics in enhancing productivity, addressing labor shortages, and fostering innovation.

Emerging markets and developing countries often face unique challenges, such as limited access to skilled labor, inadequate infrastructure, and economic volatility. However, these challenges also create a fertile ground for robotics adoption, as organizations can leverage automation to overcome barriers and drive growth. For instance, countries in Southeast Asia are witnessing a surge in robotic applications in manufacturing and agriculture, allowing them to compete more effectively on a global scale. This chapter will delve into specific opportunities in sectors such as manufacturing, agriculture, healthcare, and logistics, while also examining case studies that illustrate successful robotics integration in these regions.

5.1 Understanding Emerging Markets and Developing Countries

5.1.1 Definition of Emerging Markets

Emerging markets are typically characterized by their rapid economic growth, evolving industrial sectors, and increasing integration into the global economy. These markets, including countries in Asia, Africa, and Latin America, often exhibit higher growth rates compared to developed economies, driven by factors such as urbanization, rising consumer demand, and technological advancements.

5.1.2 Unique Characteristics of Developing Countries

Developing countries, on the other hand, may face a range of socio-economic challenges, including poverty, limited infrastructure, and insufficient access to education. Despite these challenges, many developing countries are increasingly adopting technology, including robotics, as a means to stimulate economic growth and improve living standards. For example, countries in Sub-Saharan Africa are beginning to harness robotics in agriculture to address food security and enhance productivity.

5.2 Opportunities in Manufacturing

5.2.1 Automation of Production Processes

Emerging markets are witnessing a shift towards automation in manufacturing as companies seek to enhance productivity and reduce labor costs. Robotics can play a vital role in streamlining production processes, improving quality control, and minimizing downtime. For instance, a case study of a manufacturing plant in Vietnam demonstrated that the implementation of robotic assembly lines increased production efficiency by 30% and reduced labor costs by 20%.

5.2.2 Skill Development and Workforce Transformation

The adoption of robotics in manufacturing also creates opportunities for skill development and workforce transformation. As organizations integrate automation, there is a growing demand for skilled workers who can operate and maintain robotic systems. For example, countries like India and Brazil are investing in technical training programs to equip their workforce with the necessary skills for the future job market. This investment in human capital is essential for fostering innovation and ensuring long-term economic growth.

5.2.3 Attracting Foreign Investment

The increasing adoption of robotics in manufacturing can also attract foreign investment to emerging markets. Companies seeking to expand their operations often look for regions with a skilled workforce and advanced technological capabilities. By investing in robotics infrastructure, countries can position themselves as attractive destinations for foreign investors. For instance,

Mexico has seen a rise in foreign direct investment (FDI) in its manufacturing sector, driven by its adoption of automation technologies.

5.3 Opportunities in Agriculture

5.3.1 Enhancing Agricultural Productivity

Robotics presents significant opportunities for enhancing agricultural productivity in emerging markets. Countries facing challenges such as labor shortages, land degradation, and climate change can leverage robotic technologies to optimize agricultural practices. For example, precision agriculture, which utilizes robotic systems for planting, monitoring, and harvesting crops, has been successfully implemented in countries like Kenya and Brazil, leading to increased yields and reduced resource consumption.

5.3.2 Addressing Food Security Challenges

As the global population continues to grow, food security becomes a pressing concern, particularly in developing countries. Robotics can play a critical role in addressing this challenge by improving efficiency in food production and distribution. Automated farming equipment, drones for monitoring crop health, and robotic harvesters can help farmers maximize their output and reduce waste. A notable example is the use of drones in rice production in the Philippines, which has enabled farmers to monitor crop health more effectively and improve yields.

5.3.3 Sustainable Practices and Resource Management

Robotic technologies also facilitate the adoption of sustainable agricultural practices. By utilizing robotics for tasks such as precision irrigation and targeted pest control, farmers can minimize resource usage and reduce environmental impact. For instance, robotic systems that monitor soil moisture levels can optimize irrigation schedules, conserving water and improving crop health.

5.4 Opportunities in Healthcare

5.4.1 Improving Healthcare Delivery

Emerging markets face significant challenges in healthcare delivery, including limited access to medical facilities and a shortage of healthcare professionals. Robotics can help bridge this gap by improving the efficiency and accessibility of healthcare services. For example, telepresence robots are being used in remote areas to connect patients with healthcare providers, allowing for timely consultations and diagnostics.

5.4.2 Enhancing Surgical Procedures

The adoption of robotic-assisted surgical systems is gaining traction in emerging markets, allowing for more precise and minimally invasive procedures. Countries such as India and Brazil are increasingly investing in robotic surgery programs to enhance patient outcomes and reduce recovery times. For instance, a case study of a robotic surgery program in India reported a significant reduction in complication rates and improved patient satisfaction.

5.4.3 Training and Skill Development in Healthcare

Robotics also presents opportunities for training and skill development in the healthcare sector. Simulators and robotic training systems can provide healthcare professionals with hands-on experience, enhancing their skills and knowledge. This investment in education is vital for ensuring that healthcare workers are well-equipped to utilize robotic technologies effectively.

5.5 Opportunities in Logistics

5.5.1 Automation of Supply Chain Operations

The logistics sector in emerging markets is poised for significant transformation through the adoption of robotics. Automation of supply chain operations can enhance efficiency, reduce lead times, and improve customer satisfaction. For example, the implementation of autonomous vehicles in warehouses has been shown to streamline order fulfillment processes, leading to faster delivery times and lower operational costs.

5.5.2 Addressing Urbanization Challenges

As urbanization continues to accelerate in emerging markets, logistics systems face increasing pressure to meet the demands of growing populations. Robotics can help address these challenges by optimizing last-mile delivery processes and improving traffic management. For instance, companies in China are experimenting with drone delivery systems to reach remote areas and alleviate congestion in urban centers.

5.5.3 Enhancing Inventory Management

Robotics also offers opportunities for enhancing inventory management in logistics. Automated inventory systems can provide real-time data on stock levels, reducing the risk of overstocking or stockouts. This is particularly beneficial for small and medium-sized enterprises (SMEs) that may struggle with inventory control. A case study of an SME in South Africa highlighted how the adoption of automated inventory management systems resulted in improved accuracy and reduced operational costs.

5.6 Conclusion

The opportunities presented by robotics in emerging markets and developing countries are vast and varied. By leveraging automation technologies, these regions can enhance productivity, address labor shortages, and foster innovation across various sectors. From manufacturing and agriculture to healthcare and logistics, robotics offers transformative solutions that can drive economic growth and improve living standards.

To capitalize on these opportunities, it is crucial for governments, businesses, and educational institutions to collaborate in investing in infrastructure, skill development, and regulatory frameworks that support the adoption of robotics. As the global demand for automation continues to rise, emerging markets and developing countries have the potential to become leaders in the robotics revolution, driving innovation and shaping the future of work.

Chapter 10: Future Trends in the Robotics Industry

1. Innovations on the Horizon
2. The Role of Robotics in Smart Cities
3. Predictions for the Future of Robotics Technology
4. The Impact of Artificial Intelligence and IoT on Robotics
5. Sustainability and the Future of Robotics in Society

Chapter 10

Future Trends in the Robotics Industry

Introduction

As the robotics industry continues to evolve, it is poised at the forefront of technological innovation, shaping the future of various sectors and society as a whole. This chapter will explore the emerging trends that are expected to redefine robotics in the coming years, highlighting key innovations and advancements that promise to enhance the capabilities of robotic systems.

In an increasingly interconnected world, the integration of robotics with technologies such as artificial intelligence (AI) and the Internet of Things (IoT) is set to revolutionize industries ranging from manufacturing to healthcare, transportation, and beyond. Smart cities will emerge as a significant arena for robotic applications, with intelligent systems designed to optimize urban living and improve quality of life for residents.

Additionally, this chapter will discuss the sustainability initiatives within the robotics sector, emphasizing the importance of developing eco-friendly robotic solutions that minimize environmental impact. As society grapples with pressing issues such as climate change and resource depletion, robotics will play a crucial role in driving sustainable practices across various industries.

Through examining these trends and innovations, this chapter aims to provide insights into the future landscape of the robotics industry, highlighting the potential challenges and opportunities that lie ahead. By understanding these dynamics, stakeholders can better prepare for a future where robotics becomes an integral part of daily life, enhancing productivity, efficiency, and sustainability in our increasingly complex world.

1. Innovations on the Horizon

The field of robotics is at a transformative stage, driven by rapid technological advancements and an increasing demand for automation across various industries. Innovations in robotics are not just enhancing existing capabilities but are also paving the way for entirely new applications that were once considered futuristic. This section delves into the cutting-edge innovations on the horizon, exploring key developments that promise to redefine the landscape of robotics in the coming years.

1.1. Advances in Artificial Intelligence and Machine Learning

Artificial Intelligence (AI) and Machine Learning (ML) are fundamentally changing how robots perceive and interact with their environments. Robots equipped with advanced AI algorithms can learn from their experiences, allowing them to adapt their behaviors based on changing circumstances.

For example, **Boston Dynamics' Spot robot** uses AI to navigate complex environments autonomously. By employing machine learning techniques, Spot can learn to avoid obstacles and optimize its movement patterns over time. As AI technology continues to evolve, we can expect robots to handle increasingly complex tasks, from autonomous navigation in unpredictable settings to advanced decision-making in dynamic scenarios.

1.2. Collaborative Robots (Cobots)

The emergence of collaborative robots, or cobots, is a significant innovation that enhances human-robot collaboration in various work environments. Unlike traditional industrial robots, which operate independently and often require safety cages, cobots are designed to work alongside humans, enhancing productivity without compromising safety.

For instance, **Universal Robots** has developed a range of cobots that can assist in manufacturing processes, such as assembly, painting, and quality control. These robots are equipped with sensors that allow them to detect human presence and adjust their movements accordingly, making them safe for shared workspaces. As more industries adopt cobots, we will likely see increased efficiency and reduced labor costs.

1.3. Soft Robotics

Soft robotics is an emerging field focused on creating robots with flexible, adaptable structures, enabling them to perform delicate tasks that traditional rigid robots cannot. This innovation is particularly relevant in sectors like healthcare and agriculture, where precision and gentleness are essential.

A notable example is the **Soft Robotics Gripper**, which can handle fragile items like fruits and vegetables without damaging them. By mimicking the flexibility of biological organisms, soft robots can adapt to various shapes and sizes, making them ideal for applications in environments where traditional robots would struggle.

1.4. Robotic Process Automation (RPA)

Robotic Process Automation (RPA) is revolutionizing business operations by automating repetitive, rule-based tasks that were once performed by humans. RPA tools can interact with digital systems, performing tasks like data entry, invoice processing, and customer support.

Companies like **UiPath** and **Automation Anywhere** are leading the charge in this field, providing organizations with the tools to automate workflows and improve efficiency. As RPA technology matures, we can expect broader adoption across industries, leading to increased productivity and cost savings.

1.5. Autonomous Vehicles

The development of autonomous vehicles is one of the most exciting innovations in the robotics field. Self-driving cars, trucks, and drones are set to transform transportation and logistics, offering the potential for safer and more efficient movement of goods and people.

Companies such as **Waymo** and **Tesla** are at the forefront of autonomous vehicle technology, employing advanced sensors, AI algorithms, and extensive data analysis to navigate complex environments safely. As regulatory frameworks evolve and public acceptance increases, autonomous vehicles could become a common sight on roads, revolutionizing personal and commercial transportation.

1.6. Internet of Things (IoT) Integration

The integration of robotics with the Internet of Things (IoT) is another significant innovation. IoT devices enable robots to communicate with each other and with other smart devices, creating interconnected systems that enhance efficiency and data exchange.

For example, **Amazon's robotic fulfillment centers** utilize IoT technology to optimize inventory management and order processing. Robots in these centers communicate with one another and with the warehouse management system, ensuring efficient operation and timely deliveries. As IoT technology continues to expand, the synergy between robots and connected devices will enable smarter, more efficient systems across various sectors.

1.7. Biomechanics and Bio-inspired Robotics

Research in biomechanics and bio-inspired robotics aims to develop robots that mimic the movement and efficiency of living organisms. By studying the mechanics of animal movement, engineers can design robots that are more agile, efficient, and capable of navigating challenging terrains.

A prominent example is the **MIT Cheetah robot**, which is designed to run and leap like a real cheetah, achieving impressive speeds. Innovations in bio-inspired robotics can lead to advancements in areas such as search and rescue operations, where robots need to traverse difficult environments.

1.8. Environmental Sustainability in Robotics

As the world grapples with climate change and environmental degradation, innovations in robotics are increasingly focusing on sustainability. Robotic solutions are being developed to address environmental challenges, such as waste management and renewable energy production.

For instance, **robotic waste sorting systems** are being implemented in recycling facilities to improve the efficiency and accuracy of waste separation. These systems utilize advanced vision and sorting technologies to identify and categorize materials, significantly reducing contamination rates and increasing recycling efficiency.

Conclusion

The innovations on the horizon in the robotics industry are vast and varied, encompassing advancements in AI, soft robotics, collaborative systems, and autonomous technologies. As these developments continue to unfold, they will shape the future of robotics, creating new opportunities for enhancing productivity, improving safety, and addressing global challenges. The integration of robotics into everyday life promises not only to transform industries but also to redefine how humans interact with machines, paving the way for a more automated and efficient future.

2. The Role of Robotics in Smart Cities

As urbanization continues to accelerate globally, the concept of smart cities has emerged as a promising solution to the challenges posed by rapid population growth, resource scarcity, and environmental sustainability. Smart cities leverage technology to enhance the quality of life for residents, optimize resource use, and improve urban infrastructure. Robotics plays a pivotal role in this transformation, providing innovative solutions to various aspects of city management and daily life. This section explores the multifaceted contributions of robotics in the development and operation of smart cities, highlighting key applications and examples that illustrate their potential impact.

2.1. Autonomous Transportation

One of the most visible applications of robotics in smart cities is the development of autonomous transportation systems. Self-driving vehicles, drones, and robotic shuttles are being integrated into urban transport networks to enhance mobility and reduce congestion.

For instance, **Waymo**, a subsidiary of Alphabet Inc., is testing its autonomous taxi service in cities like Phoenix, Arizona. These self-driving cars utilize advanced sensors and artificial intelligence to navigate complex urban environments safely. By reducing the reliance on personal vehicles, autonomous transportation can alleviate traffic congestion, lower emissions, and improve overall urban mobility.

2.2. Robotic Waste Management

Effective waste management is a critical challenge for cities striving for sustainability. Robotics offers innovative solutions for waste collection, sorting, and recycling processes, making them more efficient and environmentally friendly.

For example, the city of **San Francisco** has implemented robotic systems for sorting recyclables at its waste processing facilities. These robots use computer vision and machine learning algorithms to identify different materials and separate them for recycling. By automating this process, cities can improve recycling rates, reduce contamination, and minimize landfill usage.

2.3. Infrastructure Monitoring and Maintenance

Robotics is increasingly being employed to monitor and maintain urban infrastructure, ensuring that roads, bridges, and utilities remain in optimal condition. Drones and robotic inspection systems are utilized to perform regular assessments and detect issues before they become critical.

In **Barcelona**, drones are used to monitor the condition of infrastructure, including bridges and buildings. Equipped with high-resolution cameras and sensors, these drones can identify structural weaknesses and assess the need for repairs. This proactive approach not only enhances safety but also reduces maintenance costs by addressing problems early.

2.4. Public Safety and Security

The integration of robotics in public safety and security is another vital aspect of smart cities. Robotic systems can assist law enforcement, emergency services, and disaster response teams in various ways, improving overall safety for residents.

For instance, **Knightscope** has developed autonomous security robots that patrol public spaces and monitor for unusual activity. These robots are equipped with cameras and sensors to detect potential threats, providing real-time data to law enforcement agencies. By deploying these robots in high-traffic areas, cities can enhance security and reduce crime rates.

2.5. Urban Agriculture and Food Production

As cities grapple with food security and sustainability challenges, robotics is being utilized to develop urban agriculture solutions. Robotic systems can optimize food production in urban settings, utilizing limited space more effectively.

Vertical farming is one such example, where robotics and automation are used to cultivate crops in controlled environments. Companies like **Plenty** and **AeroFarms** are pioneering vertical farming techniques that utilize robotics to automate planting, monitoring, and harvesting processes. These systems can significantly increase food production while minimizing water and land usage, contributing to more sustainable urban living.

2.6. Smart Energy Management

Robotics is also playing a critical role in optimizing energy management in smart cities. Automated systems can monitor energy consumption, identify inefficiencies, and help manage the integration of renewable energy sources.

For example, **Google's DeepMind** has collaborated with **Alphabet's energy division** to develop AI-driven algorithms that optimize energy usage in data centers. These innovations can be extended to smart city applications, enabling efficient energy management in buildings and public infrastructure, ultimately reducing energy consumption and greenhouse gas emissions.

2.7. Citizen Engagement and Service Delivery

The incorporation of robotics in smart cities extends to enhancing citizen engagement and service delivery. Robots and automated systems can facilitate communication between city authorities and residents, improving access to information and services.

For instance, in **Tokyo**, interactive robots have been deployed in public spaces to provide information and assistance to residents and tourists. These robots can answer questions, offer directions, and provide real-time updates on city services, enhancing the overall citizen experience and fostering a sense of community.

2.8. Disaster Response and Recovery

Robotics has significant potential in disaster response and recovery efforts in smart cities. Automated systems can assist in search and rescue operations, assess damage, and facilitate recovery processes after natural disasters.

For example, **robots equipped with sensors and cameras** can be deployed in disaster-stricken areas to conduct reconnaissance missions. In the aftermath of earthquakes or floods, these robots can navigate hazardous environments to locate survivors and provide critical data to emergency responders, improving response times and saving lives.

Conclusion

The integration of robotics into smart cities presents a transformative opportunity to enhance urban living, improve sustainability, and optimize resource management. From autonomous transportation and waste management to public safety and citizen engagement, robotics is poised to play a crucial role in shaping the future of urban environments. As technology continues to evolve, cities that embrace these innovations will be better equipped to address the challenges of urbanization and create more livable, efficient, and resilient communities.

3. Predictions for the Future of Robotics Technology

The field of robotics has experienced unprecedented growth and innovation over the past few decades, transforming industries, enhancing everyday life, and reshaping our understanding of technology's role in society. As we look to the future, it is essential to consider how advancements in robotics technology will continue to evolve and influence various aspects of our lives. This section will explore key predictions for the future of robotics technology, examining emerging trends, potential applications, and the challenges that may arise as robots become increasingly integrated into our daily routines and industries.

3.1. Advances in Artificial Intelligence and Machine Learning

The integration of artificial intelligence (AI) and machine learning (ML) with robotics is expected to drive significant advancements in the capabilities of robots. As these technologies evolve, robots will become more adept at learning from their environments, adapting to new situations, and performing complex tasks with minimal human intervention.

For example, **Boston Dynamics' Spot robot**, which is equipped with advanced AI algorithms, can navigate various terrains, avoid obstacles, and perform tasks autonomously. In the future, we can expect robots to possess even more sophisticated cognitive abilities, allowing them to operate in dynamic environments such as homes, offices, and hospitals, and to learn from their interactions with humans and other robots.

3.2. Increased Autonomy in Robotics

As technology progresses, we will see a shift towards greater autonomy in robotics, enabling machines to perform tasks without constant human supervision. This trend will be particularly evident in industries such as manufacturing, logistics, and agriculture, where autonomous robots can operate continuously and efficiently.

For instance, **Amazon's robotic fulfillment centers** utilize autonomous mobile robots to transport goods throughout their warehouses. In the coming years, we can anticipate a broader adoption of autonomous systems in logistics, including delivery drones and self-driving vehicles, enhancing efficiency and reducing operational costs.

3.3. Collaborative Robotics and Human-Robot Interaction

The future of robotics technology will likely see an increase in collaborative robots, or "cobots," designed to work alongside humans. These robots will be equipped with advanced sensors and AI to facilitate safe and efficient interactions with human workers in various environments.

A prime example is **Universal Robots**, which produces collaborative robots that can be easily programmed to perform various tasks, such as assembly, packaging, and quality control. In the future, we can expect more intuitive human-robot interactions, allowing for seamless collaboration in sectors such as manufacturing, healthcare, and retail.

3.4. Robotics in Healthcare

The healthcare sector is poised to benefit significantly from advancements in robotics technology. We can anticipate the development of more sophisticated robotic surgical systems, rehabilitation robots, and telepresence robots that improve patient care and surgical outcomes.

For example, the **da Vinci Surgical System** has revolutionized minimally invasive surgery, allowing surgeons to perform complex procedures with precision. Future innovations may lead to fully autonomous surgical robots capable of performing operations with minimal human oversight, thereby enhancing surgical efficiency and reducing recovery times for patients.

3.5. Robotics in Education and Training

As robotics technology advances, its applications in education and training are expected to expand. Educational institutions will increasingly integrate robotics into curricula, providing students with hands-on experience and fostering skills relevant to the future job market.

Robotic kits and programming platforms, such as **LEGO Mindstorms** and **VEX Robotics**, are already popular in schools, encouraging creativity and problem-solving among students. In the future, we can expect more sophisticated educational robots capable of adaptive learning, offering personalized instruction and real-time feedback to students.

3.6. Robotics in Agriculture

The agricultural sector will continue to embrace robotics technology to improve productivity, sustainability, and efficiency. Advances in robotics will enable farmers to automate various tasks, from planting and harvesting to monitoring crop health.

For instance, **automated tractors** and **drones equipped with imaging technology** are already being used to optimize planting and irrigation practices. As these technologies advance, we can expect fully autonomous farming systems capable of managing entire operations with minimal human intervention, enhancing food security and reducing environmental impact.

3.7. Ethical Considerations and Regulations

As robotics technology advances, ethical considerations and regulatory frameworks will become increasingly important. Policymakers will need to address issues related to privacy, safety, and the impact of robotics on employment.

For instance, as autonomous vehicles become more common, discussions around liability in the event of accidents will intensify. Additionally, the integration of robots into everyday life may raise concerns about data privacy and the potential for surveillance. Future regulations will need to strike a balance between fostering innovation and ensuring public safety and ethical standards.

3.8. Robotics in Smart Cities

The integration of robotics into the development of smart cities will continue to grow, enhancing urban infrastructure, transportation, and public services. As cities become more connected, robotics technology will play a critical role in improving efficiency and sustainability.

For example, **smart waste management systems** that utilize robotic collection and sorting can optimize waste disposal processes in urban areas. In the future, we can anticipate the deployment of various robotic solutions, including autonomous public transportation systems and robotic assistants for urban planning and maintenance.

3.9. Environmental Applications of Robotics

Robotics technology will play a crucial role in addressing environmental challenges and promoting sustainability. Robots will increasingly be utilized for tasks such as environmental monitoring, pollution cleanup, and wildlife conservation.

For instance, underwater drones are being used to monitor ocean health and track marine wildlife. As environmental awareness grows, we can expect to see more innovations in robotics aimed at mitigating climate change and preserving natural ecosystems.

3.10. Conclusion

The future of robotics technology is poised for remarkable advancements that will significantly impact various sectors and aspects of daily life. From increased autonomy and collaboration to applications in healthcare and agriculture, robotics will continue to shape our world in profound ways. However, as we embrace these innovations, it is essential to address ethical considerations and regulatory challenges to ensure that the benefits of robotics are realized responsibly and equitably. The coming years promise to be an exciting time for the robotics industry, with the potential to revolutionize how we live, work, and interact with technology.

4. The Impact of Artificial Intelligence and IoT on Robotics

The integration of Artificial Intelligence (AI) and the Internet of Things (IoT) has fundamentally transformed the field of robotics, enhancing the capabilities of robots and broadening their applications across various sectors. As AI technologies continue to advance, robots are becoming more intelligent, adaptive, and efficient, enabling them to perform complex tasks and make autonomous decisions. Additionally, the IoT facilitates seamless connectivity between robots and other devices, allowing for real-time data exchange and improved operational efficiency. This section explores the profound impact of AI and IoT on robotics, highlighting the synergies between these technologies and their implications for industries, society, and future developments.

4.1. Enhanced Decision-Making Capabilities

One of the most significant impacts of AI on robotics is the enhancement of decision-making capabilities. With the integration of AI algorithms, robots can process vast amounts of data, analyze complex environments, and make informed decisions in real time. This capability is crucial for applications where rapid responses are necessary, such as in autonomous vehicles and industrial automation.

For example, **Waymo's self-driving cars** utilize AI to interpret data from sensors, cameras, and radar to navigate complex urban environments. These vehicles can detect obstacles, understand traffic signals, and anticipate the actions of pedestrians and other drivers, enabling safe and efficient autonomous driving.

4.2. Machine Learning for Improved Performance

Machine learning, a subset of AI, allows robots to learn from experience and improve their performance over time. By analyzing historical data and adapting to new information, robots can refine their algorithms to enhance efficiency and accuracy.

For instance, **Amazon's Kiva robots** in fulfillment centers use machine learning algorithms to optimize inventory management and improve the speed of order fulfillment. These robots learn from previous tasks to navigate warehouse layouts more efficiently, reducing operational costs and delivery times.

4.3. IoT Connectivity and Data Sharing

The IoT enables robots to connect with other devices, systems, and the cloud, facilitating real-time data sharing and communication. This connectivity enhances the functionality of robots, allowing them to gather data from their environment and share insights with other machines and systems.

For example, **smart manufacturing environments** employ IoT-enabled robots that communicate with sensors and machines on the production floor. This connectivity allows for predictive maintenance, where robots can monitor their own health and notify operators when maintenance is required, minimizing downtime and improving productivity.

4.4. Collaborative Robots and Human Interaction

The integration of AI and IoT has also paved the way for the development of collaborative robots (cobots) designed to work alongside humans. These robots are equipped with advanced sensors and AI algorithms that enable safe and effective interactions with human workers.

For instance, **Rethink Robotics' Baxter robot** can collaborate with human operators in manufacturing settings, learning from human actions and adapting to varying tasks. The IoT facilitates communication between Baxter and other machines, allowing for seamless coordination in the production process.

4.5. Predictive Analytics and Maintenance

The combination of AI and IoT allows for predictive analytics in robotics, enabling organizations to anticipate issues and optimize performance. By collecting and analyzing data from robotic systems, organizations can identify patterns and potential failures before they occur.

For example, **GE's Predix platform** leverages IoT data from industrial machines, including robots, to predict maintenance needs and improve operational efficiency. This proactive approach reduces downtime, extends the lifespan of equipment, and lowers maintenance costs.

4.6. Autonomous Systems and AI Algorithms

The integration of AI in robotics has led to the development of autonomous systems capable of functioning independently in dynamic environments. These systems rely on AI algorithms to interpret data from sensors and make decisions without human intervention.

For example, **DJI's Phantom drones** utilize AI algorithms for object recognition and navigation, allowing them to autonomously follow targets and perform tasks such as aerial photography and surveying. As AI continues to advance, we can expect even more sophisticated autonomous systems that can adapt to complex scenarios.

4.7. Real-Time Monitoring and Control

IoT technology provides real-time monitoring and control capabilities for robotic systems. By collecting and analyzing data from various sources, organizations can make informed decisions regarding operational efficiency and resource allocation.

For instance, **robotic lawn mowers** equipped with IoT sensors can monitor grass growth and weather conditions, allowing them to optimize mowing schedules and energy usage. This real-time monitoring ensures that resources are utilized efficiently, resulting in cost savings and improved performance.

4.8. Security and Privacy Considerations

The integration of AI and IoT in robotics raises important security and privacy concerns. As robots become more interconnected and autonomous, ensuring the security of data and systems becomes paramount. Vulnerabilities in IoT networks can be exploited by malicious actors, potentially compromising robotic systems and the data they handle.

For example, **cybersecurity incidents involving IoT devices**, such as the Mirai botnet attack, highlight the importance of securing interconnected systems. Organizations must implement robust security measures to protect robotic systems from cyber threats and safeguard sensitive data.

4.9. Ethical Implications of AI in Robotics

As AI technologies are increasingly integrated into robotics, ethical considerations come to the forefront. Issues such as accountability, transparency, and the potential for bias in AI algorithms must be addressed to ensure responsible deployment of robotic systems.

For instance, the use of AI in autonomous weapons systems raises ethical dilemmas regarding the potential for unintended harm and the need for human oversight. Establishing ethical guidelines and regulatory frameworks is essential to navigate these challenges and ensure the responsible use of AI in robotics.

4.10. Conclusion

The impact of AI and IoT on robotics is profound and far-reaching, shaping the future of industries and transforming the way we interact with technology. Enhanced decision-making capabilities, improved performance through machine learning, and seamless connectivity are just a few of the ways these technologies are revolutionizing robotics. As we move forward, addressing security, privacy, and ethical considerations will be critical to harnessing the full potential of AI and IoT in robotics, ensuring that these innovations contribute positively to society and enhance our quality of life.

5. Sustainability and the Future of Robotics in Society

As society increasingly confronts the challenges of climate change, resource depletion, and social inequality, sustainability has emerged as a critical consideration in all sectors, including robotics. The future of robotics is intrinsically linked to sustainable practices that not only enhance efficiency but also contribute positively to the environment and society. This section explores how robotics can play a pivotal role in achieving sustainability goals, examining innovative applications, technological advancements, and ethical considerations that shape the future of robotics in a sustainable society.

5.1. The Role of Robotics in Sustainable Development

Robotics has the potential to significantly contribute to sustainable development across various sectors, including agriculture, manufacturing, healthcare, and waste management. By improving efficiency, reducing resource consumption, and minimizing waste, robotic technologies can help address pressing environmental and social challenges.

For instance, **agricultural robots**, such as autonomous tractors and drones, optimize resource use by precisely applying fertilizers and pesticides only where needed, reducing chemical runoff and enhancing crop yields. This not only increases productivity but also mitigates the environmental impact of farming.

5.2. Energy Efficiency and Resource Management

Robotic systems can enhance energy efficiency in various industries by automating processes and optimizing resource management. For example, **robotic process automation (RPA)** in manufacturing can streamline production processes, reducing energy consumption and minimizing waste.

Additionally, **smart buildings** equipped with robotic systems can manage energy use more effectively. For instance, automated HVAC (heating, ventilation, and air conditioning) systems can adjust temperature settings based on occupancy and weather conditions, leading to substantial energy savings.

5.3. Robotics in Renewable Energy

The integration of robotics in renewable energy production is crucial for advancing sustainability. Robotics can enhance the efficiency of renewable energy systems, such as solar and wind power, through automation and monitoring.

For example, **solar panel cleaning robots** automate the maintenance of solar panels, ensuring optimal performance by removing dust and debris that can hinder energy production. Similarly, **drones** are increasingly used for inspecting wind turbines, allowing for timely maintenance and ensuring that these renewable energy sources operate efficiently.

5.4. Waste Management and Recycling

Robotic technologies play a vital role in improving waste management and recycling processes. Advanced robotic systems equipped with AI can automate sorting processes at recycling facilities, improving the accuracy and efficiency of material recovery.

For example, **AMP Robotics** has developed AI-powered robotic systems that can identify and sort recyclable materials from waste streams with high precision. This innovation not only increases recycling rates but also reduces the amount of waste sent to landfills.

5.5. Sustainable Manufacturing Practices

The robotics industry is moving toward more sustainable manufacturing practices by adopting eco-friendly materials and processes. Manufacturers are increasingly focused on minimizing their carbon footprint and reducing waste in production.

For instance, **3D printing technology** allows for additive manufacturing, where materials are added layer by layer, reducing material waste compared to traditional subtractive manufacturing methods. Robots can automate the 3D printing process, ensuring precision and efficiency.

5.6. Ethical Considerations in Sustainable Robotics

As robotics technology advances, ethical considerations surrounding sustainability become increasingly important. The development and deployment of robots should prioritize environmental protection, social equity, and ethical labor practices.

For example, ensuring that robotic systems are designed with energy efficiency in mind and that their production processes do not contribute to environmental degradation is crucial. Additionally, addressing the potential impact of automation on employment and ensuring equitable access to robotic technologies are vital ethical considerations.

5.7. The Future of Work and Sustainability

The future of work is likely to be significantly influenced by robotics and automation, presenting both opportunities and challenges for sustainability. While robotics can enhance productivity and efficiency, there are concerns about job displacement and the need for workforce reskilling.

For instance, as industries increasingly adopt robotic technologies, workers may need to acquire new skills to adapt to changing job roles. Investing in education and training programs that focus on robotics and sustainable practices can help ensure that the workforce is prepared for the future.

5.8. Policy and Regulation for Sustainable Robotics

The development of policies and regulations that promote sustainable robotics practices is essential for ensuring that robotic technologies contribute positively to society and the environment. Governments and organizations should establish frameworks that encourage innovation while prioritizing sustainability.

For example, regulatory bodies can incentivize companies to adopt eco-friendly manufacturing practices, invest in sustainable technologies, and engage in corporate social responsibility initiatives. These measures can help create a more sustainable robotics industry.

5.9. Public Perception and Acceptance of Robotics

The successful integration of robotics into society also depends on public perception and acceptance. Educating the public about the benefits of robotics for sustainability can help foster a positive attitude toward these technologies.

For instance, community engagement initiatives that showcase the environmental benefits of robotic technologies in agriculture and waste management can enhance public understanding and support for sustainable robotics.

5.10. Conclusion

The intersection of robotics and sustainability presents significant opportunities for advancing environmental protection, resource efficiency, and social equity. As robotic technologies continue to evolve, their potential to contribute to sustainable development becomes increasingly apparent. By addressing ethical considerations, investing in workforce training, and establishing supportive policies, society can harness the power of robotics to create a more sustainable future. The collaboration between technology and sustainability will play a crucial role in shaping the future of robotics in society, ultimately contributing to a healthier planet and a better quality of life for all.

Conclusion

- Summary of Key Insights from the Robotics Industry
- Final Thoughts on the Future of Robotics
- Call to Action for Industry Stakeholders
- The Importance of Collaboration in the Robotics Ecosystem
- Encouraging Innovation and Ethical Practices in Robotics

Conclusion

Summary of Key Insights from the Robotics Industry

The robotics industry has undergone significant transformation over the past few decades, evolving from basic automation tools to sophisticated systems integrated with artificial intelligence and advanced sensors. Key insights highlight the crucial role of robotics across various sectors, including manufacturing, healthcare, agriculture, and logistics. As companies increasingly adopt robotics to enhance efficiency and productivity, the landscape of industries continues to change, driven by innovations in technology and shifting consumer demands.

Final Thoughts on the Future of Robotics

Looking ahead, the future of robotics appears promising yet complex. Emerging technologies such as artificial intelligence, machine learning, and the Internet of Things (IoT) are poised to further enhance robotic capabilities, enabling them to perform more intricate tasks and operate in dynamic environments. However, the rapid evolution of robotics also raises questions about ethics, regulation, and the potential impacts on the workforce. Stakeholders must remain vigilant and proactive in addressing these challenges to harness the full potential of robotics.

Call to Action for Industry Stakeholders

Industry stakeholders, including manufacturers, policymakers, and researchers, must collaborate to drive the development and adoption of robotics. A call to action is essential for creating standards and regulations that foster innovation while ensuring safety and ethical considerations. Engaging with the broader community, including educational institutions and public organizations, can facilitate knowledge sharing and promote the responsible advancement of robotics.

The Importance of Collaboration in the Robotics Ecosystem

Collaboration is vital in the robotics ecosystem, as it fosters innovation and accelerates the pace of development. Partnerships between private companies, academic institutions, and government agencies can lead to groundbreaking research and applications that address societal challenges. By working together, stakeholders can create an environment conducive to innovation while ensuring that the benefits of robotics are accessible to all.

Encouraging Innovation and Ethical Practices in Robotics

Encouraging innovation in robotics is crucial for the industry's growth, but it must be accompanied by a commitment to ethical practices. As robotics technology advances, stakeholders should prioritize transparency, accountability, and inclusivity. By integrating ethical considerations into the design, development, and deployment of robotic systems, the industry can build trust with users and society at large, ensuring that robotics serves as a tool for positive change.

In conclusion, the robotics industry stands at a pivotal juncture, with immense opportunities and challenges ahead. By embracing collaboration, prioritizing ethical practices, and fostering innovation, we can pave the way for a future where robotics enhances lives and contributes to a sustainable and equitable society.

References

References

1. ABB Group. (n.d.). Robotics. Retrieved from ABB Robotics

2. ABB Robotics. (n.d.). Robotics & Discrete Automation. Retrieved from ABB

3. Advanced Robotics for Manufacturing (ARM) Institute. (n.d.). "About ARM." Retrieved from ARM Institute.

4. Agility Robotics. (2023). "Digit: The Future of Bipedal Robots." Retrieved from Agility Robotics

5. Aiken, D. (2020). The Impact of Cyber Attacks on Robotics in Manufacturing. *Journal of Cybersecurity Research*, 5(2), 45-60.

6. Alavi, M., & Sadeghi, M. (2021). "Robotics in Smart Cities: The Future of Urban Living." *International Journal of Urban Sciences.*

7. Al-Sharif, L., et al. (2020). "Energy Harvesting Technologies for Autonomous Robots." *IEEE Transactions on Industrial Electronics*, 67(9), 7598-7607.

8. Amazon Prime Air. (2022). *Delivering the Future: Amazon's Drone Delivery Service.* Retrieved from Amazon

9. Amazon Robotics. (2021). *How Robots Are Transforming Logistics and E-commerce.*

10. Amazon Robotics. (2022). *Amazon's Robotics Revolution: Improving Fulfillment and Delivery.* Retrieved from Amazon

11. Amazon Robotics. (2023). "Working with MIT: Innovating for Efficiency." Retrieved from Amazon Robotics

12. Arntz, M., Gregory, T., & Zierahn, U. (2016). *The Risk of Automation for Jobs in OECD Countries: A Comparative Analysis.* OECD Social, Employment and Migration Working Papers, No. 189, OECD Publishing, Paris.

13. Asimov, Isaac. *I, Robot.* New York: Gnome Press, 1950.

14. Babbage, Charles. *Passages from the Life of a Philosopher.* London: Longman, 1864.

15. BCG. (2020). *The New Normal: How COVID-19 is Accelerating Digital Transformation.*

16. Bekey, G. A. (2005). *Robot Ethics: The Ethical and Social Implications of Robotics.* IEEE Technology and Society Magazine, 24(1), 2-15.

17. Bhatia, A., & Mehta, H. (2020). "Robotic Surgery: A Review of Current Applications and Future Perspectives." *Journal of Robotic Surgery*, 14(4), 703-708.

18. Binns, R. (2018). Fairness in Machine Learning: Lessons from Political Philosophy. *Proceedings of the 2018 Conference on Fairness, Accountability, and Transparency*, 149-158.

19. Bishop, C. M. (2006). *Pattern Recognition and Machine Learning*. Springer.

20. Blanchard, S. (2019). *Robotics: The Next Generation*. Springer.

21. Bogue, R. (2018). "An Overview of Soft Robotics." *Industrial Robot: An International Journal*, 45(1), 12-17.

22. Bogue, R. (2018). "Collaborative Robots: A Review of Current Developments and Future Prospects." *Industrial Robot: An International Journal*, 45(5), 584-589.

23. Bogue, R. (2018). "Robotic safety: A review of the current state of the art." *Industrial Robot: An International Journal*, 45(3), 383-392.

24. Bogue, R. (2018). "Robotics: a review of the current state of the art." *Industrial Robot: An International Journal*.

25. Bogue, R. (2018). "The Industrial Internet of Things: Opportunities and Challenges". *Industrial Robot: An International Journal*, 45(5), 550-557.

26. Bogue, R. (2018). "What are the developments in industrial robots?" *Industrial Robot: An International Journal*, 45(1), 9-14.

27. Bogue, R. (2018). "Service robots: a review of recent developments." *Industrial Robot: An International Journal*, 45(5), 669-673.

28. Bogue, R. (2018). "Service robots: a review of recent developments." *Industrial Robot: An International Journal*, 45(5), 669-673.

29. Bogue, R. (2018). "Service robots: a review of recent developments." *Industrial Robot: An International Journal*, 45(5), 669-673.

30. Bogue, R. (2020). "Exoskeletons: A review of current research and applications." *Industrial Robot: An International Journal*, 47(5), 609-615.

31. Bogue, R. (2021). "Robotics for smart cities: An overview." *Industrial Robot: An International Journal*.

32. Bogue, R. (2022). "The Future of Robotics: Trends and Predictions." *Industrial Robot: An International Journal*.

33. Bogue, R. (2023). "Sustainability in Robotics: Innovations and Future Directions." *Industrial Robot: An International Journal*.

34. Bogue, R. (2023). "The Impact of AI and IoT on Robotics." *Industrial Robot: An International Journal*.

35. Borenstein, J., Herst, C., & Koren, Y. (1996). "The Vector Field Histogram for Mobile Robot Navigation." *IEEE Transactions on Robotics and Automation*, 7(3), 278-288.

36. Boston Consulting Group (BCG). (2022). *How Robotics Will Impact Global Manufacturing*.

37. Boston Consulting Group. (2020). *The New Normal: How COVID-19 is Accelerating Digital Transformation.*

38. Boston Dynamics. (2021). *Stretch: A Robot Designed for Warehouse Logistics.* Retrieved from Boston Dynamics

39. Boston Dynamics. (2023). "Our Partners." Retrieved from Boston Dynamics

40. Boston Dynamics. (2024). "Robotic Systems Overview." Retrieved from Boston Dynamics website.

41. Boston Dynamics. (n.d.). "Atlas." Retrieved from Boston Dynamics.

42. Brambilla, M., et al. (2013). "Swarm robotics: a review from the swarm engineering perspective." *Swarm Intelligence*, 7(1), 1-41.

43. Breazeal, C. (2004). "Social Interactions in Human-Robot Interaction." *Human-Robot Interaction: A New Paradigm for Interactive Systems*, 1-10.

44. Brooks, R. (1986). "A Robust Layered Control System for a Mobile Robot." *IEEE Conference on Robotics and Automation.*

45. Brooks, R. (1991). "Intelligence without Reason." *Proceedings of the 12th International Joint Conference on Artificial Intelligence.*

46. Brooks, R. (1999). "Cambrian Intelligence: The Early History of the New AI." MIT Press.

47. Brooks, R. A. (2002). "Human-Level AI's Killer Application: Interactive Unmanned Ground Vehicles." *AI Magazine*.

48. Bruno, M. (2019). *Robotics and Automation Handbook*. CRC Press.

49. Brynjolfsson, E., & McAfee, A. (2014). *The Second Machine Age: Work, Progress, and Prosperity in a Time of Brilliant Technologies*. W.W. Norton & Company.

50. Bryson, J. J. (2018). The ethical and legal implications of autonomous machines. AI & Society, 33(4), 591-598.

51. Cacace, J. (2020). "Design and Prototyping for Robotics: A Study of Industrial Applications." *Journal of Robotics and Automation* 15(3), 102-113.

52. Čapek, Karel. *R.U.R. (Rossum's Universal Robots)*. Prague: Aventinum, 1920.

53. Carnegie Mellon University Robotics Institute. (n.d.). "Tartan Racing." Retrieved from CMU Robotics Institute.

54. Chui, M., Manyika, J., & Miremadi, M. (2016). "Where machines could replace humans—and where they can't (yet)." *McKinsey Quarterly*.

55. Chui, M., Manyika, J., & Miremadi, M. (2016). *Where machines could replace humans—and where they can't (yet)*. McKinsey Quarterly.

56. Chui, M., Manyika, J., & Miremadi, M. (2020). "The Future of Work: How Technology is Reshaping the Workforce." *McKinsey Global Institute.*

57. Chui, M., Manyika, J., & Miremadi, M. (2022). "The Internet of Things: How AI is Transforming Robotics." *McKinsey Global Institute.*

58. Coppelia Robotics. (2020). "V-REP: The Robot Simulation Software." Retrieved from Coppelia Robotics website.

59. Coyle, J. (2020). "Robotics in Manufacturing: Trends and Innovations." *Manufacturing Engineering,* 164(2), 28-35.

60. Craig, J. J. (2005). *Introduction to Robotics: Mechanics and Control.* Pearson.

61. Cummings, M. L. (2021). "Artificial Intelligence and Robotics: Predictions for the Future." *AI & Society.*

62. Dando, J. (2020). "Autonomous vehicles in smart cities: Implications for transportation." *Transport Policy.*

63. Dario, P., & Siciliano, B. (2016). "Assistive Robotics: Designing for Usability and Acceptance." *Journal of Robotics and Autonomous Systems.*

64. Dautenhahn, K., & Saunders, J. (2016). "The Role of Social Robots in the Development of Social Skills." *International Journal of Social Robotics*, 8(1), 1-12.

65. Decker, A. (2019). "The Future of Robotics: A Guide for Decision Makers." *Automation World.*

66. Defense Advanced Research Projects Agency (DARPA). (n.d.). "DARPA Robotics Challenge." Retrieved from DARPA Robotics Challenge.

67. Deloitte. (2022). *The Economic Impact of Robotics: How Automation is Reshaping Global Markets.*

68. Devol, G. & H. G. (1961). "Programmed Article." United States Patent Office.

69. Devol, George. *Unimate: The First Industrial Robot.* New York: Unimation, 1954.

70. DHL Supply Chain. (2022). "Sustainable Logistics: The Role of Robotics." Retrieved from DHL

71. DHL Supply Chain. (2022). "The Future of Logistics: Robotics in Supply Chain." Retrieved from DHL

72. Dignum, V. (2018). "Responsible Artificial Intelligence: Designing AI for Human Values." *Proceedings of the 2018 AAAI/ACM Conference on AI, Ethics, and Society,* 1-6.

73. Dignum, V. (2019). Responsible Artificial Intelligence: Designing AI for Human Values. *ITU Journal: ICT Discover,* 1(1), 1-10.

74. DJI. (2024). "Drones and Innovative Materials." Retrieved from DJI website.

75. Duffy, B. R. (2003). Anthropomorphism and the social robot. In Proceedings of the 2003 IEEE International Conference on Robotics and Automation (Vol. 3, pp. 13-18).

76. Duffy, Brian R. "The Social Robot." *Robotics and Autonomous Systems* 42, no. 3 (2003): 177-190.

77. Ekso Bionics. "Robotic Exoskeletons for Mobility Rehabilitation." Ekso Bionics, 2019.

78. Engelberger, Joseph. *Robotics in Practice: Future Prospects for Industrial Robots*. MIT Press, 1980.

79. European Commission. (2018). European Strategy on Robotics. [Link]

80. European Commission. (2019). "Ethics Guidelines for Trustworthy AI." Retrieved from Ethics Guidelines for Trustworthy AI.

81. European Commission. (2021). Proposal for a Regulation laying down harmonised rules on artificial intelligence (Artificial Intelligence Act). [Link]

82. European Commission. (2021). White Paper on Artificial Intelligence: A European approach to excellence and trust. [Link]

83. European Commission. (n.d.). "Horizon 2020." Retrieved from European Commission.

84. European Union. (2016). General Data Protection Regulation (GDPR). [Link]

85. Fanuc Corporation. (n.d.). Company Profile. Retrieved from Fanuc

86. Fanuc Corporation. (n.d.). Industrial Robots. Retrieved from Fanuc

87. Fanuc Corporation. (n.d.). Industrial Robots. Retrieved from Fanuc

88. Fischer, J. E., & Tschinkel, H. (2016). "Robots with Emotional Intelligence: A Review of the Current State and Future Directions." *International Journal of Social Robotics*, 8(1), 1-12.

89. Flynn, J. (2021). Privacy and Data Security in the Age of AI and Robotics: A Global Perspective. *International Journal of Information Management*, 61, 102362.

90. Fong, T., et al. (2003). "The Human-Robot Interaction: An Overview." *IEEE Robotics & Automation Magazine*, 10(1), 28-36.

91. Frank, M. (2021). "Collaborative Robots: The Future of Automation." *Robotics Business Review.*

92. Franklin, G. F., & Powell, J. D. (2010). *Feedback Control of Dynamic Systems*. Pearson.

93. Future of Life Institute. (2017). Asilomar AI Principles. [Link]

94. Gans, J. (2021). "Cloud Robotics: Current status and future trends." *Robotics and Autonomous Systems*, 145, 103866.

95. Government of Japan. (2015). "Robot Revolution Initiative." Retrieved from Robot Revolution Initiative.

96. Government of Singapore. (n.d.). "Smart Nation Initiative." Retrieved from Smart Nation.

97. Grand View Research. (2021). *Robotics Market Size, Share & Trends Analysis Report By Type, By Application, By Region, And Segment Forecasts, 2021 - 2028.*

98. Groover, M. P. (2013). *Industrial Robotics: Technology, Programming, and Applications.* McGraw-Hill.

99. Groover, M. P. (2015). *Industrial Robotics: Technology, Programming, and Applications.* McGraw-Hill.

100. Gude, A. (2020). "The Future of Automated Manufacturing." *Automation World.* Retrieved from Automation World.

101. Gude, A. (2020). "The Future of Automated Manufacturing." *Automation World.* Retrieved from Automation World.

102. Gurumurthy, R., & Jayakrishna, M. (2019). "Recent Trends in Robotics Manufacturing." *Journal of Manufacturing Technology Management.*

103. Huang, Y., & Liu, L. (2020). "Soft Robotics: A New Frontier in Robotics." *Journal of Bionic Engineering.*

104. Hurst, J. (2019). "The Use of Robotic Exoskeletons in Rehabilitation." *Rehabilitation Robotics*, 2(1), 45-50.

105. Hwang, H., et al. (2019). "Collaborative Robots: An Introduction and Overview." *Journal of Industrial Information Integration*, 15, 1-7.

106. International Federation of Robotics (IFR). (2022). "Robotics and Sustainable Development: A Global Perspective." *IFR Reports.*

107. International Federation of Robotics (IFR). (2022). *World Robotics Report 2022.*

108. International Federation of Robotics (IFR). (2023). "World Robotics Report 2023." Retrieved from IFR

109. International Federation of Robotics (IFR). (2023). World Robotics Report 2023.

110. International Federation of Robotics. (2021). *World Robotics 2021.*

111. International Organization for Standardization (ISO). (n.d.). "ISO 10218 - Robots and robotic devices." Retrieved from ISO 10218.

112. International Organization for Standardization (ISO). Robotics Standards.

113. Intuitive Surgical. (2021). *da Vinci Surgical System.* Retrieved from Intuitive Surgical

114. Intuitive Surgical. (2021). *The da Vinci Surgical System.*

115. iRobot Corporation. (n.d.). "Roomba." Retrieved from iRobot.

116. iRobot Corporation. (n.d.). Company Overview. Retrieved from iRobot

117. iRobot. "Roomba: Revolutionizing Household Chores with Robotics." iRobot, 2002.

118. iRobot. (2024). "Robotic Innovations and Sustainability." Retrieved from iRobot website.

119. ISO 10218-1:2011. (2011). *Robots and robotic devices – Safety requirements for industrial robots – Part 1: Robots*. International Organization for Standardization.

120. Ivanov, S., & Webster, C. (2021). "The Role of Robotics in Urban Agriculture." *Journal of Urban Technology*.

121. Japan Cabinet Office. (2015). New Robot Strategy: The Japanese Government's Strategy for Promotion of Robotics Technology. [Link]

122. Japan Industrial Robotics Association (JARA). Japan's Robotics Strategy. [Link]

123. Kahn, J. (2018). Robots and the Future of Healthcare: Challenges and Opportunities. *Health Affairs*, 37(12), 2052-2058.

124. Kahn, P. (2013). "The Future of Robotics: An Overview." *Journal of Robotics*, 2013, 1-14.

125. Kato, H., & Arai, T. (2018). "Innovative Robotics: Advances in Manufacturing Techniques." *Robotics and Computer-Integrated Manufacturing*.

126. Korean Ministry of Trade, Industry and Energy. (2020). Korea Robot Industry Development Plan. [Link]

127. Kormushev, P., Ghadirian, H., & Panuccio, G. (2013). "Robot Learning from Demonstration: A

Survey." *Journal of Robotics and Autonomous Systems*, 61(2), 122-134.

128. KPMG. (2022). "Harnessing the Power of IoT and AI in Robotics." *Global Technology Report*.

129. KUKA AG. (n.d.). Company Overview. Retrieved from KUKA

130. Kuka Robotics. (2020). "The Future of Robotics." Retrieved from KUKA

131. KUKA Robotics. (2022). *KUKA Robotics: Solutions for Industrial Automation*. Retrieved from KUKA

132. KUKA. (n.d.). Robotics. Retrieved from KUKA Robotics

133. Kuo, B. C. (2009). *Automatic Control Systems*. Wiley.

134. Kwon, O. (2018). "Human-Robot Interaction: A survey of current research." *Frontiers in Robotics and AI*, 5, 1-12.

135. LeCun, Y., Bengio, Y., & Haffner, P. (1998). "Gradient-Based Learning Applied to Document Recognition." *Proceedings of the IEEE*, 86(11), 2278-2324.

136. Lee, J. K., & Kim, Y. (2020). "Robotic Rehabilitation: Enhancing Outcomes for Patients with Neurological Disorders." *Journal of NeuroEngineering and Rehabilitation*, 17(1), 85.

137. Lin, P., Abney, K., & Bekey, G. A. (2012). Robot ethics: The ethical and social implications of robotics. Cambridge, MA: MIT Press.

138. MarketsandMarkets. (2022). Consumer Robotics Market by Type, Application, and Region - Global Forecast to 2028.

139. MarketsandMarkets. (2022). *Robotics Market by Type, Application, and Region - Global Forecast to 2028.*

140. MarketsandMarkets. (2022). *Robotics Market by Type, Application, and Region - Global Forecast to 2028.*

141. Mataric, M. J. (2007). "The Robotics of Human-Robot Interaction." *IEEE Intelligent Systems*, 22(5), 24-29.

142. McKinsey & Company. (2020). "How AI is Reshaping Supply Chain Management." Retrieved from McKinsey

143. McKinsey & Company. (2021). "The Future of Robotics in Logistics." Retrieved from McKinsey

144. McKinsey & Company. (2021). How AI is Changing the Landscape of Robotics Adoption.

145. McKinsey & Company. (2021). *The Future of Work After COVID-19: Implications for Robotics and Automation.*

146. McKinsey & Company. (2021). *The Future of Work After COVID-19: Implications for Robotics and Automation.*

147. McKinsey & Company. (2021). *The Future of Work: How Robots Will Change Employment.*

148. McKinsey & Company. (2022). "The Future of Robotics: Strategic Partnerships in a New Era." Retrieved from McKinsey

149. McKinsey & Company. (2023). "Robotics: The Next Wave of Startups." Retrieved from McKinsey

150. McKinsey Global Institute. (2017). *A Future That Works: Automation, Employment, and Productivity.*

151. McKinsey Global Institute. (2021). *The Future of Work: Rethinking Skills to Tackle the UK's Workforce Crisis.*

152. MIT Media Lab. (n.d.). "Kismet: The Robot That Knows Emotions." Retrieved from MIT Media Lab.

153. Müller, J. (2022). "The Role of Robotics in Achieving Sustainability Goals." *Sustainable Robotics Review.*

154. Murphy, R. R. (2000). *Human-Robot Interaction in Rescue Robotics.* Springer.

155. NASA. "Mars Exploration Rover Mission: Spirit and Opportunity." NASA, 2004.

156. NASA. (n.d.). "Robotics." Retrieved from NASA Robotics.

157. National Institute of Standards and Technology. (2019). Framework for Cybersecurity in Smart Manufacturing. [Link]

158. National Institute of Standards and Technology. (2021). AI Risk Management Framework. [Link]

159. National Science Foundation. (n.d.). "Robotics Program." Retrieved from NSF Robotics Program.

160. Ocado Group. (2021). *How Ocado Uses Robotics to Optimize Its Grocery Business*. Retrieved from Ocado

161. O'Reilly, J. (2017). "Biohybrid robots: Combining biology and robotics." *Journal of The Royal Society Interface*, 14(128), 20170381.

162. Paden, B., et al. (2016). "A Survey of Motion Planning Techniques for Self-Driving Urban Vehicles." *IEEE Transactions on Intelligent Vehicles*, 1(1), 33-49.

163. Panuwatwanich, K., & Suttipun, M. (2020). "The impact of robotics on the logistics industry." *International Journal of Logistics Systems and Management*, 35(4), 467-485.

164. PrecisionHawk. (2021). *Drones in Agriculture: How Drones Are Used in Farming*.

165. Pugh, S. (1991). *Total Design: Integrated Methods for Successful Product Engineering*. Addison-Wesley.

166. Pugh, S. (1991). *Total Design: Integrated Methods for Successful Product Engineering*. Addison-Wesley.

167. PwC. (2020). *The Future of the Logistics Industry: Trends and Opportunities*.

168. PwC. (2021). *Will Robots Really Steal Our Jobs? An Analysis of the Future of Employment.*

169. PwC. (2022). Consumer Attitudes Toward Robotics: Opportunities and Challenges.

170. Quigley, M., et al. (2009). "ROS: An open-source Robot Operating System." In *ICRA Workshop on Open Source Software.*

171. Raji, I. D., & Buolamwini, J. (2019). Actionable Auditing: Investigating the Impact of Publicly Naming Biased Performance Results of Commercial AI Products. *Proceedings of the 2019 AAAI/ACM Conference on AI, Ethics, and Society.*

172. Ransbotham, S., & Mitra, S. (2020). "Disaster Response Robots: The Future of Emergency Services." *Journal of Disaster Research.*

173. Research and Markets. (2021). Global Robotics Market: Growth, Trends, COVID-19 Impact, and Forecasts (2022 - 2028).

174. Riaz, T., & Ahsan, S. (2021). "Future Directions in Robotic Surgery and Rehabilitation." *International Journal of Surgery*, 88, 20-25.

175. Robot Report. (2023). "Emerging Startups in Robotics: A Look at the Future." Retrieved from Robot Report

176. Robot Report. (2023). "The Growing Importance of Strategic Partnerships in Robotics." Retrieved from Robot Report

177. Robotic Industries Association (RIA). (2022). "The Role of AI and IoT in Robotics." *Industry Reports.*

178. Robotic Industries Association (RIA). (2023). "Robotics: A Global Perspective." *Industry Reports.*

179. Rojas, R. (2017). "Soft Robotics: Trends, Applications, and Future Directions." *Frontiers in Robotics and AI*, 4, 25.

180. Rojas, R. (2019). "Artificial Intelligence in Robotics: Applications and Challenges." *International Journal of Advanced Robotic Systems*, 16(4), 1729881419863455.

181. Rosenberg, A., & Matusik, W. (2016). "The Future of Robotics: What Will it Mean for Us?" *MIT Technology Review.*

182. Rus, D., & Tolley, M. T. (2015). "Design, fabrication and control of soft robots." *Nature*, 521(7553), 467-475.

183. Russell, S., & Norvig, P. (2010). *Artificial Intelligence: A Modern Approach.* Pearson.

184. Scheinman, V. (1973). "The Stanford Arm." Stanford University.

185. Scheinman, Victor. "Development of the Stanford Arm." *Stanford Robotics Institute Journal*, 1969.

186. Shalev-Shwartz, S., & Ben-David, S. (2014). "Understanding Machine Learning: From Theory to Algorithms." Cambridge University Press.

187. Shishika, M. M., & Bhat, A. R. (2020). "A Review on Advanced Materials in Robotics." *International Journal of Engineering Research & Technology*.

188. Siciliano, B., & Khatib, O. (2008). *Springer Handbook of Robotics*. Springer.

189. *Handbook of Robotics*. Springer.

190. Siciliano, B., & Khatib, O. (2016). *Springer Handbook of Robotics*. Springer.

191. *Handbook of Robotics*. Springer.

192. Singh, A., & Dutta, A. (2021). "Advancements in Robotic Technologies for Sustainable Manufacturing." *Journal of Cleaner Production*.

193. Starship Technologies. (2022). "Robotic Delivery Solutions for Urban Environments." Retrieved from Starship

194. Starship Technologies. (2023). "Autonomous Delivery Robots: Revolutionizing Last-Mile Delivery." Retrieved from Starship Technologies

195. State Council of the People's Republic of China. (2016). "Robotics Industry Development Plan." Retrieved from Robotics Industry Development Plan.

196. Statista. (2022). Consumer Robotics - Statistics & Facts.

197. Statista. (2022). *Robotics Industry - Statistics & Facts*.

198. Statista. (2022). *Robotics Industry - Statistics & Facts.*

199. Tesla, Inc. "Autonomous Driving Technology and the Future of Mobility." Tesla, 2016.

200. The World Bank. (2021). *Robotics in Agriculture: Opportunities and Challenges.*

201. Thrun, S., & Burgard, W. (2005). *A Probabilistic Approach to Robot Mapping. The International Journal of Robotics Research*, 25(5-6), 457-463.

202. Thrun, S., Burgard, W., & Fox, D. (2005). *Probabilistic Robotics*. MIT Press.

203. Thrun, S., Burgard, W., & Fox, D. (2005). *Probabilistic Robotics*. MIT Press.

204. Toh, S. H., & Chen, J. (2021). "Logistics Robotics: Trends and Developments." *Logistics*, 5(3), 32.

205. Tschiesner, A., et al. (2021). *How to Adopt Automation and Robotics in the Manufacturing Industry*. McKinsey & Company.

206. Tzeng, J. H. (2020). "The Rise of Robotics in Agriculture: A Comprehensive Review." *Agricultural Robotics*, 1(1), 1-15.

207. U.S. Department of Transportation. (2020). Automated Vehicles 4.0: A Regulatory Framework for Automated Vehicles.

208. UK Government. (n.d.). "UK Robotics and Autonomous Systems (RAS) Strategy." Retrieved from UK RAS Strategy.

209. United Nations. (2021). *World Population Prospects 2021*.

210. Universal Robots. (n.d.). Collaborative Robots. Retrieved from Universal Robots

211. Universal Robots. (n.d.). Company Information. Retrieved from Universal Robots

212. Varma, A., & Jain, S. (2019). "The Impact of Robotics in Manufacturing." *Journal of Manufacturing Technology Management*, 30(4), 659-674.

213. Waymo. (2021). *Waymo's Autonomous Delivery Vehicles: The Future of Transportation*. Retrieved from Waymo

214. West, D. M. (2020). "The Future of Work: Robots, AI, and Automation." *Brookings Institution Press*.

215. Wiener, Norbert. *Cybernetics and the Human Brain*. Boston: MIT Press, 1965.

216. Wiener, Norbert. *Cybernetics: Or Control and Communication in the Animal and the Machine*. New York: MIT Press, 1948.

217. Wise, David J. *Robotics and Artificial Intelligence: A Reference Guide*. Santa Barbara: ABC-CLIO, 2001.

218. World Economic Forum (WEF). (2023). "The Future of Work in a Robotics-Driven Economy." *Global Reports on Robotics and Automation*.

219. World Economic Forum. (2020). *The Future of Jobs Report 2020.*

220. World Economic Forum. (2022). *The Future of Jobs Report 2022.*

221. Yanco, H. A., & Drury, J. L. (2004). "Classifying Human-Robot Interaction: An Efficient Framework." *Proceedings of the 2004 IEEE International Conference on Robotics and Automation.*

222. Yandell, K. (2021). "The Role of Robotics in a Sustainable Future." *Robotics and Autonomous Systems.*

223. Yang, Y., & Li, J. (2020). "Robotics in Healthcare: A Review of Applications and Challenges." *Healthcare Technology Letters*, 7(2), 47-53.

224. Yaskawa Electric Corporation. (n.d.). Robotics. Retrieved from Yaskawa

225. Zebra Technologies. (2021). "Mobile Robotics: Transforming Warehouse Operations." Retrieved from Zebra

226. Zeng, Y., et al. (2020). "Modular Robotics: A Review." *Robotics and Autonomous Systems*, 132, 103-123.

www.ingramcontent.com/pod-product-compliance
Lightning Source LLC
LaVergne TN
LVHW051430050326
832903LV00030BD/3007